The Child and the State

The Child & the State

A Normative Theory of Juvenile Rights

LAURENCE D. HOULGATE

THE JOHNS HOPKINS UNIVERSITY PRESS
Baltimore and London

This book was brought to publication with the generous assistance of the Andrew W. Mellon Foundation.

Manufactured in the United States of America

The Johns Hopkins University Press, Baltimore, Maryland 21218
The Johns Hopkins Press Ltd., London

Library of Congress Catalog Card Number 79–15393
ISBN 0–8018–2288–2

Library of Congress Cataloging in Publication data will be found on the last printed page of this book.

For Torre

To turn [a child] loose to an unrestrained liberty, before he has reason to guide him, is not allowing him the privilege of his nature to be free, but to thrust him out amongst brutes, and abandon him to a state as wretched and as much beneath that of a man as theirs. This is that which puts the authority into the parents' hands to govern the minority of their children.

John Locke, the second of the
Two Treatises on Government

The basic right of a juvenile is not to liberty, but to custody.

Ex parte Crouse, 4 Whart. 9,
11 (Sup. Ct. Pa. 1839)

The child's happiness, too, is willed by the Deity; the child, too, has faculties to be exercised; the child, too, needs scope for the exercise of those faculties; the child therefore has claims to freedom—rights as we call them—coextensive with those of the adult. We cannot avoid this conclusion, if we would. Either we must reject the law altogether, or we must include under it both sexes and all ages.

Herbert Spencer, *Social Statics*

Constitutional rights do not mature and come into being magically only when one attains the state-defined age of majority; minors, as well as adults, are protected by the Constitution and possess constitutional rights.

Planned Parenthood of Missouri
v. *Danforth,* 428 U.S. 52 (1976)

Contents

Preface xi
Acknowledgments xv

Part 1 The Need for a Theory 1

1 Introduction: Rights and Principles 3
The Nature of Rights 6
Legal Rights 9
Normative Principles 10
A Philosophical Problem of Children's Rights 15
2 The Legal Status of the Child 17
Positive Claim Rights 17
Negative Claim Rights 20
Liberties 22
Mixed Rights: Liberties/Powers 26
Mixed Rights: Due Process 28
Immunities 29
Summary 31
3 The Child As a Person: Recent Supreme Court Decisions 33
The First Amendment: *Tinker* and *Ginsberg* 34
The Right of Privacy: *Danforth* and *Carey* 37
The Right to Due Process: *In re Gault* 39
Conclusion 41

Part 2 Toward a Theory of Juvenile Rights 45

4 Two Arguments from Moral Agency 47
The Argument from "Actual" Moral Agency 50
Discussion of the Argument 52
The Argument from "Potential" Moral Agency 56
Moral Rights and Potential Persons 58
Conclusion 59
5 Beneficence and Rational Choice 61
Clarification of the Argument 62

The Principle of Beneficence 64
The Capacity for Rational Choice 66
Do Children Lack the Capacity for Rational Choice? 68
Conclusion 72
6 The Argument from Utility 74
Direct Effects of Paternalism 75
Side Effects of Paternalism 78
The Principle of Utility 79
Conclusion 81
7 The Argument from the Social Contract 83
The Justification of Principles of Justice 83
The Social Contract and Paternalism 85
Criticisms of the Argument 87

Part 3 A Theory of Juvenile Rights 93

8 Outline of a Theory 95
The Concept of Justice in Distribution 97
Distributing Liberty and Claim Rights 100
Conclusion 102
9 Goods and Needs 104
Happiness, Goods, and Interests 104
Weighing Interests: Principles of "Practicality" 108
Needs and Justice 110
Justice and Paternalism 114

Part 4 Applications of the Theory 117

10 Status Offenses 119
Review of the Current Debate 119
Analysis of the Debate 121
Applying the Theory 122
Conclusion 126
11 Child Neglect 129
Review of the Current Debate 130
Analysis of the Debate 131
Applying the Theory 132
Conclusion 134
12 Rehabilitation and Justice 138
Preliminary: The Nature and Justification of Rehabilitation 138
Rehabilitation, Illness, and the Juvenile Offender 144
Conclusion and Recommendations 148

Notes 155
Index 161

Preface

There is an 1874 case that is widely known among social workers as "the Mary Ellen affair." The case is about an abused child in New York City and a remarkable woman who attempted to intervene in the child's behalf. The social worker discovered, however, that there was no law making it illegal to neglect or abuse a child. So, with an extraordinary bit of ingenuity, she went to the Society for the Prevention of Cruelty to Animals and persuaded them to prosecute the parents of the child under the existing cruelty to animals law, arguing that since children are of the animal species, they too have a right not to be subjected to cruel treatment by anyone, including their parents. The prosecution was successful, the child was saved, and the publicity stimulated child neglect legislation throughout the United States.

There is an interesting parallel in academic philosophy to this priority of concern about animals and children. The last few years have seen a spate of philosophical interest in the rights of animals, as evidenced by a number of books, at least one anthology, and several journal articles, most of them arguing for the proposition that we ought to accord certain moral and legal rights to members of animal species different from our own. But social philosophers have been strangely silent about the rights of children. Although some philosophers in the modern period made brief attempts to address the topic (e.g., Locke, Mill, Spencer), it has been generally ignored by contemporary philosophers. Indeed, most of the recent theorizing on children's rights has been left to lawyers, educators, and sociologists. I think that this is unfortunate, for surely the most important questions to ask about the rights of children are *normative*. Since social (and political) philosophy is concerned to present, develop, and analyze general normative principles or criteria for answering moral questions of public policy, then social philosophers are perhaps better prepared than most to answer normative questions about the legal rights of children.

There is an obvious practical need for a normative theory of juvenile rights. Legal rights are granted or denied to children in a fragmentary way. There is little evidence of attempts by legal scholars to provide a theory of rights upon which decisions about the legal rights that children ought to possess can be based. Existing theories are either (1) simplistic defenses of the present legal status of children or (2) polemical attacks on this status, followed by proposals for radical legal reform. Such defenses, attacks, or proposals are rarely argued for in the context of plausible normative principles that the author consciously puts forward for critical examination. Hence, legislators and judges (who have to make the system work) must operate either with these existing materials or with a confusing and often incoherent set of intuitions of the following sort: children somehow (it is not clear how) "belong" to their parents and ought not to be given any legal rights that will conflict with the original rights of the parent; children are "persons" or "potential persons" and thus have at least some moral rights that a legal system ought to recognize; or else children are "incompetent" and thus need to be protected from harming themselves. And somehow all of these views have to be controlled by the dictates of the social or general welfare. In the face of this, it is not surprising that changes in the laws regarding children's rights are made haphazardly. Philosophers should be able to provide a better foundation for legal change than what now exists.

It is the aim of this book to provide such a foundation—a "normative theory of juvenile rights." I do this by analyzing the relevant distinctions with regard to legal rights per se, describing the current legal status of children in the light of these distinctions, critically discussing relevant Supreme Court decisions, and making a careful assessment of the traditional arguments for denying certain legal rights to children while granting them others. By doing these things in the first two parts of the book I aim to clear the way for a coherent theory.

In the concluding parts of the book I describe and then defend a specific general theory. Roughly, the line of justification I adopt is one that employs the moral principle of utility and mediates this with the principle of equalitarian justice. After a detailed defense of the general theory, I argue for a number of specific recommendations for change in current juvenile law. The arguments, of course, serve the additional purpose of providing illustration of the general theory. First, I argue that only those children who clearly lack the capacity for rational choice (a concept defined in an earlier chapter), ought to have their liberty restricted by so-called juvenile status offenses, and then only by a much smaller and precisely defined number of such offenses than is currently found in most state statutes. Second, child neglect statutes should be revised to allow state intervention on the basis of parental neglect of children only in cases where a child's "basic needs" are not being met by the parents. A standard of "basic needs" is suggested to guide legislators in constructing specific permissible areas for state intervention. Finally, I urge that we abandon rehabilitation as the overriding aim of the juvenile court. I suggest new guidelines for the adjudication phase of delinquency proceedings and I make specific suggestions for the sort of response that the state ought to make to juveniles who have been adjudicated delinquent.

I regard my book as only *one* attempt to construct and defend a normative theory of juvenile rights. It is my hope that, like the Mary Ellen affair, it will at least stimulate some interest among my colleagues in what I regard as an immensely rich and important area of philosophical inquiry. If it accomplishes nothing else, I shall regard my endeavor as well worth the effort.

Acknowledgments

Parts of chapters 5 and 6 of this book appear in "Children, Paternalism and Rights to Liberty," in *Having Children: Philosophical and Legal Reflections on Parenthood,* ed. Onora O'Neill and William Ruddick for the Society for Philosophy and Public Affairs (New York: Oxford University Press, 1979). I should like to thank the editors and Oxford University Press for permission to reprint parts of this essay.

Major funding for the writing phase of this book came from a stipend granted me by the National Endowment for the Humanities. I am also indebted to the American Council of Learned Societies, the George Mason University Foundation, and the School of Law of the University of Virginia for providing the material support that allowed me to study juvenile law and do basic research for the book during the academic year 1976/77. The Chautauqua Institution and the administrators of Smith Library (particularly Mrs. Torrey Isaac) provided a quiet and lovely place in which to work during the summers of 1977 and 1978.

I owe a considerable debt to Professor Lawrence Becker of Hollins College and to Professor Carl Wellman of Washington University (St. Louis). Their thorough critiques of earlier drafts of this manuscript saved me from many mistakes. Of course, I assume sole responsibility for any errors that may remain.

Finally, I should like to give special thanks to Mrs. May Thompson for her patient and careful typing of several drafts of the entire manuscript, and to William P. Sisler and Wendy A. Harris of The Johns Hopkins University Press for invaluable encouragement and editorial assistance throughout the latter stages of manuscript preparation.

Part 1
The Need for a Theory

1 Introduction: Rights and Principles

In his entertaining introduction to a recent anthology of essays on children's rights, the late Paul Goodman observed that such essays always take contradictory tacks.[1] They argue on the one hand that children should be accorded all of the legal rights now accorded to adults: they should be allowed to vote, to make contracts, and to decide for themselves whether or not to attend school, just as adults do. On the other hand, so goes another argument, we should give children certain special rights precisely because they are children: unlike adults they should have the right to be protected from those who would exploit their labor, to be provided with a permanent and stable home environment, to have an education that will meet their individual needs, and so on. In the former case, the assumption appears to be that (most) children are as competent as many adults to make the relevant decisions. But in the latter case the argument for the claim that children should be given certain "special rights" of protection seems to be that (most) children are *not* competent to make the relevant decisions. One is left wondering how these two positions can be seriously advanced by a single author.

Some of the confusion that Goodman saw in recent recommendations for change in juvenile law is to be found in the existing body of law itself. There does not always appear to be a clearly defined principle or a consistent set of principles upon which legislative and judicial decisions about the rights of children are based. If paternalism is (roughly) defined as the principle that justifies interference in the life of another person for his or her own good, then although adherence to this principle explains much of juvenile law, there are certainly some curious anomalies. For example, paternalism may be the principle behind the legislative decision to allow children to avoid the obligations of most of their contracts, but it does not seem to explain why children are made liable for their own torts. Again, we may discern the paternalistic motives of a legislature that requires a fourteen-year-old female to obtain parental consent if she is to marry, but at the same time be unable to understand why the same principle did not persuade the Supreme Court to require her to obtain parental consent if she wishes to terminate a pregnancy by abortion. (The odd result of this recent ruling[2] is that although she is not required to get her parents' consent in order to have an abortion, she must have it before she can marry the father of the child.)

It has been said that what juvenile law needs is its own jurisprudence. However, I doubt that this would provide the solution to the preceding difficulties. In the accepted sense of the term, jurisprudence is a "science which has for its function to ascertain the principles on which legal rules are based."[3] The point I attempted to illustrate briefly above is that it is not entirely clear that there *is* a single principle or a consistent set of principles that can be said to stand behind or to explain the legislative decisions pertaining to juvenile law. But more important than this, what principles we succeed in discovering stand in need of justification. If, for example, we decide that the principle of paternalism dominates juvenile law, then we will want to ask for the justification of this principle and its application to juvenile behavior. Why is it justifiable to interfere coercively in the life of another person "for his own good"? If this is not always justifiable, then when is it? How does this apply to the particular case of children?

It is the central aim of this book to answer these questions by constructing a normative theory of juvenile legal rights. I mean by the phrase "normative theory of legal rights" a justifiable (set of) normative principle(s) that can be used to guide decision and judgment making about legal rights. Since the legal rights that are my particular concern are the rights of the class of children, then I propose to construct and defend a theory that will allow us to make reasonable decisions about the legal rights that ought to be granted or denied to members of this class.

The problem of constructing a theory of juvenile rights properly belongs to social philosophy. There is no agreed-upon definition of this rather amorphous area of inquiry. Perhaps I should say only that it deals with a large miscellaneous set of philosophical questions about social relations. Questions about the nature and justification of the relation between the child and the state clearly belong in this domain. Such questions are typically of two kinds. First, there are questions about the meaning of concepts. In my inquiries about children I shall have occasion to ask about concepts that express social ideals (for example, "justice," "equality," "beneficence"), concepts that enter into the expression of normative principles (for example, "good," "need," "interest," "harm"), and the concept that expresses the nature of the relationship between persons that is the main concern of this book: the notion of "a right."

Second, there are questions of a normative kind; for instance, By what principles are we to grant or deny legal rights to children? Joel Feinberg has suggested that when we pose normative questions such as this "it is convenient to think of [them] as questions for some hypothetical and abstract political body."[4] The answer to the preceding question would guide legislators and judges toward reasonable decisions in particularly difficult cases, for by posing normative questions the social philosopher is in effect asking what laws conferring rights would be created by an "ideally reasonable legislature." The legislature would, of course, have to be one in a community whose history, customs, and political institutions resemble our own; hence, in this book I confine myself to inquiring about the rights of children as they would ideally exist under United States law. A further clarification of this approach to the normative problem is that an "ideally reasonable legislature" is to be thought of as composed of members who are somewhat abstracted from the full legislative context in that they are "free to appeal to the public interest unencumbered by the need to please voters, to make 'deals' with colleagues, or any other merely 'political' considerations."[5] The practical importance of this is that although the actual rational legislator may not always be able to appeal merely to the principles of the ideal legislator, those principles "provide a target for our aspirations and a standard for judging our successes and failures."[6]

In order to prepare the ground for the search for these principles and for further discussion of the problem of children's rights in this and succeeding chapters, there are two preliminary questions to be posed and answered. First, I have said that my inquiry is about the legal rights of children. What, then, is a "right"? What kinds of rights are there? What makes a right "legal," rather than "moral" or "human"? Second, I have remarked that my task is to discover the normative principles that are to guide decisions about granting legal rights to children. What is a "principle"? What kinds of normative principles are there? How are they to be justified or known to be true?

In the remainder of this chapter, I shall sketch answers to these questions and then conclude with further remarks about the need for a theory of juvenile rights and the approach I shall take in the remainder of this book.

The Nature of Rights

The word "right" has multiple meanings; we would be well advised to refrain from entering into a discussion of these meanings and to proceed directly to that which is most relevant to the present concern: a definition that will specify the general nature of the relation between children as right holders and others as right regarders.[7] In fact, it was the legal writer W. N. Hohfeld who first distinguished kinds of rights with regard to this element.[8] Thus, the distinctions he drew between a right "in the strictest sense" and such other rights as liberties, powers, and immunities all specified various ways in which right holders relate to right regarders. I shall briefly indicate what is meant by each of these various kinds of "right relationships" before turning to a definition of the concept of a "legal right."

Claims. Consider, first, Hohfeld's definition of a right "in the strictest sense" of this term. Contemporary philosophers choose to refer to this as a *claim* that one individual (the right holder) has on another (the duty bearer) for an act or forbearance in the sense that "should the claim be in force or exercised, and the act or forbearance not be done, it would be moral (or legal, in the case of a legal right), other things being equal, to use coercive measures to extract either the specific performance (i.e., the act or forbearance claimed), or compensation in lieu of it."[9]

Examples of claim rights from the sphere of children's law are easy to come by. Thus, the right that a child has to be provided with a proper home, subsistence, education, medical care, and a proper moral climate is a claim right in the sense defined. The duty bearer may be either the parents or other legally responsible custodians or the state itself under the doctrine of *parens patriae*. Thus, if a child is not being provided with the aforementioned items, and he chooses to exercise his right, then the court may (it would be legal to) either order the parents (or other custodians) to improve the child's situation while the child remains at home or, in extreme cases, take the child out of the home into institutional care or a foster home either temporarily or permanently. In the extreme case, it is the state that becomes the ultimate duty bearer.

There are a number of ways of distinguishing claim rights. One distinction I have found to be extremely useful is that between *positive* and *negative* claim rights.[10] A positive right is a right to other persons' positive actions. A negative right is a right to other persons' omissions or forbearances. For example, the right of a child to be provided with whatever medical treatment is necessary for the protection of his life or limb is to be classified as a positive right. This is a right that imposes on others the duty to do something for the child. Examples of negative rights include the right not to be abused (by parent, guardian, or teacher, for example), the right to privacy, and the right to an undamaged reputation.

Lawrence Becker argues persuasively for another sort of claim right that is importantly relevant to the topic of this book. He calls it a *capacity claim,* and he describes it as follows: "One may wish, in asserting one's rights, to call particular attention to one's status as a potential holder of rights. That is, one may wish merely to assert, with a statement such as 'I have a right to get married,' that one is of age and mentally competent—that one has the legal capacity to get married."[11]

This sort of claim right can cause confusion. The confusion can be traced to the fact that "the relevant 'capacity' or 'standing' is presupposed by the existence of other sorts of rights." Someone advocating that children should have the right to make contracts or wills is at least advocating that they should have a certain power (such that if one follows the prescribed form, the will must be recognized). But he may also be advocating something more fundamental, namely, that children should have the status or standing to be the holder of rights. "Right-claim locutions come naturally here, they amount to the assertion that others 'owe' one the recognition that one has the capacity—the relevant qualifications or standing as defined by the right-making institutions or considerations—to possess one or more sorts of rights."[12] In the case of children, the relevant right-claim locution often heard in their behalf is (not that they have, but) that they *should have* the standing to possess many of the sorts of rights possessed by adults. This is one of the proposals I shall examine in detail in part 3.

Liberties (Privileges). A second class of rights—referred to by Hohfeld as "privileges," but more accurately called "liberties"—does *not* entail the existence of duties in others, but just the opposite, namely, the *absence* of duties in the ones who have the liberties, and so the *absence* of correlative claim rights in others. Thus, if A is at liberty to walk the streets at night, then this implies not that others have certain duties with respect to A but that A has no duty to refrain from being on the street and others have no claim right that A refrain from this activity. A possible confusion here is that many legal liberties are *secured* by claim rights. Thus, my legal right to walk about freely on the public streets is given legal emphasis by the enforcement of duties in others not to interfere with my exercise of that liberty. But the existence of this duty is not entailed by the mere existence of the liberty right.

Although some liberties may be "natural" (existing independently of any existing social institution), my concern in this book is with "legal" liberties. The question to be raised with regard to children is whether they ought to be granted the sorts of legal liberties that are usually granted to adults and secured for them by the relevant claim rights.

Powers. The third type of relationship that exists between right holders and others is what Hohfeld labeled a *power*. Thus, to assert that a child lacks the right to execute a will is to assert that he is unable to alter his relations with other persons in this way. That is, "the existence of a power right is the existence of a state of affairs such that one person (the right holder) may morally (or legally) alter at will some of the rights, duties, liberties, powers, or immunities of another person (the liability bearer)."[13] The contrast with liberties is obvious. If a person does what he has no liberty right to do, then his doing it is an *offense*. But if he does what he has no legal power to do, his doing it is a *nullity*, it has no legal effect. For example, to assert that a child is not at liberty to remain on the public streets between 11 p.m. and 6 a.m. implies that if he should do this then his act would be an offense. However, to say that a child has "no right to vote" is not to say that if a child votes this will constitute an offense. It is to say that if he or she should attempt to cast a ballot this act would have no legal effect: it would not be called "voting."

Immunities. Hohfeld's fourth and final type of right relationship is specified by the concept of an *immunity.* An immunity bears the same general contrast to a power that a privilege does to a (claim) right. As Hohfeld explains it, "a [claim] right is one's affirmative claim against another, and a privilege [liberty] is one's freedom from the right or claim of another. Similarly, a power is one's affirmative 'control' over a given legal relation as against another; whereas an immunity is one's freedom from the legal power or 'control' of another as regards some legal relation."[14] Thus, we sometimes say, using the language of rights, that children have the right not to have certain of their claim rights (such as to an inheritance) subject to willful alteration by their parents or other custodians. The child, that is, has an immunity, and the existence of the immunity entails a disability, a lack of power, in the parents (or custodians).

Mixed Rights. Many expressions of the form "the right to . . ." combine two or more of the kinds of rights specified by Hohfeld. For example, the right to marry is part liberty (no one has a right that you not marry) and part power (if you go through the prescribed ritual, you alter your marital status). Moreover, both the liberty and the power presuppose that you have the capacity right to exercise the liberty/power right to marry. When rights are combined under an expression of the form "the right to . . . ," I shall call it a *mixed right.*

One of the most important mixed rights discussed in this book is the right to due process. It consists of such legal rights as the right to be assisted by counsel, to a speedy trial, to a public trial, to confront opposing witnesses, to a trial by jury, to be free from double jeopardy, and to non–self-incrimination. Not only is the right to due process a mixture of rights, but some of the specified rights are combinations of kinds of rights. Thus, we find not only a liberty (the right to confront opposing witnesses), an immunity (the right to be free from double jeopardy), and claims (the right to a speedy trial, the right to a public trial), but also a right that is a mixture of liberty and claim (the right to non–self-incrimination).

Instead of breaking up my future discussions of the right to due process into discussion of its constituent kinds of rights by considering each of the latter under its "proper" heading, I will henceforth consider it as a whole under a separate grouping. My reason for this is partly because the phrase "due process" is now so much a part of our vocabulary; it is also because the question whether children ought to have the right to due process is one to which so much paper and ink has already been devoted that it would be uncharitable to break with tradition at this late stage.

Legal Rights

Lawrence Becker has argued that in addition to defining rights by exploring the sorts of relationships that obtain between the right holder and others, philosophers have often offered definitions of rights in terms of their source of justification.[15] For example, the distinction between legal and moral rights is drawn by distinguishing between the conditions under which each right claim may be said to be justified. A *legal right* is a right that is justified by an appeal to law in a given system. There is, of course, a large controversy over the question of *what* rights are matters of law. Are they those rights that the courts will, in fact, enforce (legal realism), those that the legal system ought to recognize (natural law), or those that are actually "recognized," either implicitly or explicitly, by the legal system (contemporary legal positivism)? For my own part, I lean toward the last theory of law, although I do not defend it here because it would not be relevant to the immediate task. The central question of the book is not What rights are matters of law? but What rights *ought* to be matters of law? It makes no difference whether this question is interpreted as asking what rights ought to be enforced by the courts or what rights ought to be implicitly or explicitly recognized by the legal system. I can remain neutral on the answer to this controversy.

A *moral right* is a right that is held to exist prior to, or independent of, any legal or institutional system of rules. One justifies such a right by an appeal to moral reasons. Of course, one's concept of a moral reason becomes crucial in determining what counts as a moral right. Thus, if one wants to argue that children have a moral right to medical care it is important to decide what sort of reason one is prepared to accept in moral argument. Will an argument from utility do? Justice? Prudence? Unless we decide such questions in advance, further debate is often fruitless.

Within the genus of moral rights is found the species *human rights*. A human right is generically a moral right held equally by all human beings "unconditionally and unalterably." Anyone who justifies a right claim for a particular person (or group of persons) by indicating that he is a human being and that all human beings hold that right equally is arguing that the person possesses a human right.

The notion of a human right is often used interchangeably with that of a *natural right*, and I shall follow this practice in this study. However, we should be aware that when some philosophers talk about a right's being natural they imply that the right has a certain metaphysical status (for example, it is conferred on one by God), or that it has a certain epistemic property (for example, it can be known to exist by anyone who possesses the capacity to reason).[16] I shall not imply any such claim when I make reference in future chapters to the notion of a natural right.

Although the focus of this study shall be on the legal rights of children, I will have frequent occasion to discuss claims about the moral and human rights of the child. This is because appeals to moral and/or human rights are often made to give support to the position that whereas children ought to be granted certain legal rights they ought to be denied others. In order to assess such arguments properly, it will be necessary to look carefully at these concepts and the conditions under which they can be said to apply to children.

Normative Principles

The second of my two preliminary questions has to do with the normative aspect of the problem of children's rights: What principles shall we appeal to in making decisions about granting (or denying) legal rights to children? How are we to discover these principles? Since both of these questions assume an understanding of the concept of a normative principle, I shall begin by specifying what I mean by this concept before turning to a further description of these questions.

The Nature of Normative Principles. There are two types of normative principles I shall have occasion to discuss. The first is a *legal* principle. An occasion for its use is a judicial decision. For example, the oft-quoted proposition "No one shall be permitted to profit by or take advantage of his own wrong" is a legal principle sometimes employed by the courts as a reason for settling lawsuits in a particular way. I shall show in a moment how it is to be distinguished from a legal rule. The second type of normative principle is a *moral* principle. There are several occasions for the use of such principles, but the one I shall be particularly concerned to discuss is when such principles are used to help people decide whether particular rules or principles ought to be adopted as law, that is, ought to be made legal rules or legal principles. An example of a moral principle that has this function is the (vaguely formulated) principle of beneficence "One ought to promote the good and prevent evil." This principle might function as a reason for adopting as law such rules as those prohibiting assault, fraud, or trespass.

One and the same principle can be used in a judicial, a legislative, or a noninstitutional context. A judge might decide a case a particular way because he or she accepts the principle that children ought to have their liberty restricted in order to prevent them from harming themselves. A legislator might use the same principle to justify a vote to adopt a particular law, for example, a juvenile curfew statute. And a parent might apply his or her own version of paternalism in refusing to allow a child to use the family car.

The important distinction is between (legal or moral) normative principles and legal rules. The distinction has been well drawn by Professor Ronald M. Dworkin.[17] His concern was to distinguish legal principles from legal rules, but I think that his remarks also serve to distinguish between moral principles and legal rules. First, legal rules apply in an "all or nothing fashion." If we have an accurate statement of a legal rule, including an enumeration of all of its exceptions, and we have the facts of a particular case before us, then we can stipulate that there is or is not a violation of the rule. Moral and legal principles clearly do not have this character. Thus, if I accept and use the principle of paternalism to assess a particular law, I have a reason that argues in one direction (for instance, that the proposed law should be rejected), but I cannot accurately maintain that the proposed law was a "clear violation" of the principle. This is partly because principles, unlike legal rules, do not have exceptions built into the statement of them. One version of the principle of paternalism, for example, asserts that persons ought to be prevented from doing acts that might lead to self-harm. If the proposed law gives a right to children the exercise of which might lead to self-harm, then the principle of paternalism is *a* reason I must take into account in deciding whether to support it. But it is only a reason. There may be other principles arguing in the other direction—a principle of equalitarian justice for example. If so, the principle of paternalism may not prevail, but this does not mean that I should reject it entirely as a principle of evaluation, because in the next case, when these contravening considerations (such as that of equality) are absent or less weighty, the principle of paternalism may prevail.

The second point about rules and principles to which Professor Dworkin makes reference is related to the first. Principles have a dimension of "weight and importance" not possessed by legal rules. When two principles collide (for instance, the principles of paternalism and equalitarian justice), we must resolve this conflict by deciding which principle is more important or weighty in the circumstance. But when two legal rules conflict we cannot say that one rule is more important than another within the system of rules. Rather, we say that one of them is invalid; it must be abandoned or recast. This is done by appealing to considerations beyond the rules themselves. "A legal system might regulate such conflicts by other rules, which prefer the rule enacted by the higher authority, or the rule enacted later, or the more specific rule, or something of that sort. A legal system may also prefer the rule supported by the more important principles. (Our own legal system uses both of these techniques.)"[18]

The Discovery of Normative Principles. How are we to go about discovering those "correct" normative principles that are to guide us in our attempt to lay a rational foundation for granting or denying legal rights to children? The approach I adopt in this book begins with the construction of a possible argument for denying certain rights to children. I then extract from the argument the normative principle(s) implicit in it. To take a crude example, someone may hold that it is justifiable to deny rights to children because he believes that children are not "self-legislating," and he holds to the principle that it is morally justifiable to deny rights to beings who are not self-legislating.

The next step is to test the extracted principle. There are two methods of argument that I employ. First, it is important to see whether the principle contains concepts that are blurred or incoherent. Thus, if pressed to define the concept of "self-legislating" as it is used in the preceding normative principle, one may find it hard to provide a definition that excludes children without also excluding most adults. Second, normative principles are tested by our responses that their consequences are acceptable or unacceptable. That is, I try to discover whether the extracted principle can accommodate singular moral judgments and attitudes in which we have the greatest confidence. Some general principles used in support of denying liberties to children seem to provide an equally good justification for denying them to certain classes of adults. Someone who holds such a principle but who cannot accept the consequent rightness of denying liberties to adults is trapped in an inconsistency.

If it is found that the principle cannot accommodate one or more of our confidently held singular moral judgments, then there are two options: (1) *reject* the principle and replace it with one that will accommodate the specific judgment,* or (2) *retain* the principle but show that it is *less weighty* than some other principle—in particular, the principle that is implicit in the confidently held singular moral judgment that the former principle failed to accommodate. The only important difference between these alternatives is that whereas the consistent application of option 1 leads finally to a single, fundamental normative principle, option 2 gives us a *set* of normative principles ordered in a hierarchy. In either case the end result is the same: we accommodate the singular moral judgments in which we have the greatest confidence. In the early chapters of part 2 I find it useful to attempt to find a single normative principle. However, my concluding statement in part 3 proposes a *pair* of normative principles, consistent with approach 2, only because I find this to be a somewhat clearer way of stating my own normative theory of juvenile rights. The resulting theory is then employed to deal with some perplexing borderline cases of children's rights discussed in part 4.

Types of Moral Principles. Philosophers have traditionally distinguished between two different kinds of moral principles. One kind is called *deontological*. This group of moral principles informs us that our duty is "to do that which is inherently fair or just or right, as determined

*This may simply be a revision of the rejected principle.

either by direct consideration of the act itself and its situation of itself, or by reference to some general formal principle (often one whose denial is self-contradictory)."[19] The other kind is called *teleological*. This group of principles tells us that our duty is to do what will promote the good, have the best consequences, or maximize utility.

Each group of principles can be used to deal with (moral and legal) rights but the ways in which they treat these rights are remarkably different. Consider, for example, the right not to be tortured. Most deontologists would assert this as a human right and from this "fact" *derive* the duty of others to refrain from acts of torture. The statement that there is such a duty may be called a deontological moral rule, for it tells us to refrain from doing something that it would be inherently wrong to do; but it is wrong *because* it would be in violation of a human right. In this respect the right is morally basic and the duty is derivative from it.

Teleological moral principles, on the other hand, do not derive from any kind of right. Rather, rights are derivative from these principles. "To have a right," the utilitarian John Stuart Mill argued, "is to have something which society ought to defend me in the possession of."[20] The central idea here is that rights function not to mark out some feature of humanity but rather to mark out which of all the claims a person has that society ought to enforce either by law or by education and opinion. What society *ought* to enforce is, of course, to be determined by looking to the consequences of enforcement. This is not to deny that teleologists are able to account for such things as the right not to be tortured. Thus, if one is a utilitarian one would begin by establishing (on utilitarian grounds) a duty not to torture, defining a claim right in terms of the duty, and then deriving the right from the duty.

Legal rights can be justified by both deontological and teleological principles. Indeed, both kinds of principles can be employed to justify granting the *same* legal right to a person or group of persons. Thus, we might justify the right to freedom of expression both because this is a human right and because the consequences of having the right to express oneself freely are better than the consequences of not having the right. On the other hand, since the principles that justify this are different, the rights justified by one kind of principle may well be opposed to the rights justified by the other. Thus, one might advocate that a certain class of persons be denied a liberty right on the grounds that this will maximize happiness or the general good while another might oppose this on the ground that to deny the right would be to commit an injustice. This sort of clash will be given ample illustration in the ensuing discussion of proposals to grant or deny rights to children.

A Philosophical Problem of Children's Rights

Now I want to redescribe what I take to be a central philosophical problem that must be solved by those who would make proposals for granting or denying legal rights to children. The problem is best put by attending once again to the conflicting trends described by Paul Goodman in the current rush to champion the cause of children. They are trends that not only operate from quite different factual assumptions about the emotional and cognitive capacities of children, but that often employ different moral principles in their arguments for granting them legal rights. What is so surprising is that with one or two exceptions[21] the children's rights advocates in each group have failed to see the inconsistency of their assumptions with those of the other.

In the first and by far the largest group are those who are attempting to secure more positive and negative claim rights for children. These are the "child protectionists," the people who are largely responsible for the remarkable amount of protective legislation that has been enacted on behalf of children and for making visible many of the ways in which children have been and are abused and victimized. The normative moral principle that is often (though not always) implicit in their arguments for granting more positive and negative claim rights is the teleological principle of beneficence: we have a duty to promote the good of others. Since children as a class are too weak and too limited in their emotional and cognitive capacities to help or to protect themselves, it is argued that we have an especially urgent duty to create special positive and negative claim rights for them.

In the second and smaller (but hardly less vocal) group of children's rights advocates are those who are attempting to secure more liberty and power rights for children. Their interests are in liberating the child from legal restrictions on his liberty instead of protecting him by law from those who would harm, abuse, or exploit him. But in order to make this argument for more liberties and power rights work, this group usually assigns a lower priority to principles like beneficence, for it sees them in this context to be a mere disguise for paternalism. That is, these people give less weight to teleological considerations because they see them as ultimately justifying more restrictions on a child's liberty of action ("for his own good"), calling for fewer rights to liberty than are accorded to adults. Instead, this group of child advocates ("liberationists") usually give first priority to the deontological principle of justice, understood simply as equality of treatment.

Moreover, in order to prove that children deserve equal treatment under the law, they attempt to convince others that children are indeed relevantly like adults. For if children possess relevant likenesses, then it is clear that the principle of equalitarian justice demands that they be granted all of the liberty rights now accorded to the latter group.

Although there are a number of serious questions arising from this all too brief account, the dilemma facing the children's rights movement appears to be this. If we agree with the second group of child advocates (the liberationists), then consistency seems to demand that we not only grant children all the liberty and power rights that we now grant to adults, but we must give up our attempts to have children accorded more positive and negative claim rights than we now accord to adults: justice demands it. Alternatively, if we side with the first group (the protectionists), then in the name of consistency it appears that we must not only try to have enacted legislation that will give children more positive and negative claim rights than we give to adults, but we must restrict their liberty whenever we feel that it is in their "best interests" to do so: beneficence demands it.

This book is an attempt to find a solution to this and other problems. The attempt will involve the construction and defense of a theory of juvenile rights. I will provide this in parts 2 and 3. In part 2 I examine a number of theories that have attempted to justify denying children certain legal rights to liberty. Although none of these theories succeeds, I show that the criticism of them reveals two moral principles that, when properly analyzed and weighted, provide an adequate rationale for granting or denying legal rights. This theory will be proposed in part 3, and then tested in part 4 by application to three specific problems of juvenile law.

In the remainder of part 1 I give a brief account of the legal status of children. I begin by reviewing the current status of the child in the United States law. The reader who is already acquainted with juvenile law may wish to omit this chapter, although it might be of interest to note the way in which I categorize the rights of children using the Hohfeldian distinctions set forth above. In chapter 3 I describe some of the major decisions of the U.S. Supreme Court relevant to the rights of children. My purpose is to display some of the normative legal principles at work in these decisions in order to prepare the ground for the critical inquiry to be undertaken in the remainder of the book.

2 *The Legal Status of the Child*

In the preceding chapter I distinguished several kinds of rights using Hohfeld's method of ordering rights by the kinds of relationships that obtain between right holders and right regarders. My aim in doing this was to provide the framework necessary for classifying some of the rights of children as they exist under present-day United States law. This task of classification, to which I now turn, will not only provide the reader with an overview of the present legal status of the child, but it will display the dramatic differences between the way in which the law treats the child and the treatment it accords the competent adult. Although children and competent adults share many important legal rights (for example, most of the negative claim rights guaranteed by the statutes and precedents of the criminal law), it is the contrasts between children and adults that are relevant to this study, and they shall be emphasized in this chapter.

However, I must warn the reader that my object is not to be thorough and encyclopedic. There are excellent books reporting the rights of children under U.S. law to which one can refer for a comprehensive account with annotation.[1] As noted above, I wish merely to provide a coherent overview of the legal status of the child. Accordingly, I have organized this chapter into six divisions corresponding to kinds of right relationships distinguished in chapter 1: positive claim rights, negative claim rights, liberties, mixed rights (liberties/powers and due process), and immunities.

Positive Claim Rights

The Right to Rehabilitation. If there has been progress at all in the movement to secure more rights for children in this century, evidence is surely to be found in the general area of positive claim rights, and one of the most noteworthy of such rights is the right of a child under a certain age (usually eighteen) who has violated a criminal law (or who has engaged in certain noncriminal courses of conduct) to be treated by the state in a manner much different from that accorded the adult violator. The juvenile court movement that began in the United States in the late 1800s secured for children the positive right to be *rehabilitated* by the state instead of punished for their offenses.* "According to this 'juvenile court philosophy' juvenile courts exist to help children in trouble with the law rather than simply to punish them or to make them examples, used by society, to deter others. It is fundamentally a conception which affirms that the state owes children a duty of protection and a chance of rehabilitation."[2]

As a result of securing the positive claim right correlative to the aforementioned duty, a juvenile court becomes a significantly different kind of court.

> Children are to be dealt with separately from adults. Their cases are to be heard at a different time, and preferably, in a different place; they are to be detained in separate buildings, and, if institutional guidance is necessary, they are to be committed to institutions for children. Through its probation officers the court can keep in constant touch with the children who have appeared before it. Taking children from their parents is, when possible, to be avoided; on the other hand, parental obligations are to be enforced. The procedure of the court must be as informal as possible. Its purpose is not to punish but to save. It is to deal with children not as criminals but as persons in whose guidance and welfare the State is peculiarly interested. Save in the case of adults, its jurisdiction is equitable, not criminal, in nature.[3]

Even the terminology is different from that used in a criminal proceeding. Thus, a child is not "arrested" but "apprehended" or "taken into custody" (the former term was believed to be too stigmatizing). A child whose case is "adjudicated" (never "tried") may be found to be a "delinquent" (a child

*At early common law, children "over the age of discretion" did not have the (positive) right to be treated any differently from the way the state would treat an adult in the event that they should commit a criminal act. The age of discretion was fixed at seven years. Children of less than seven years could not be punished as criminals. Children between the ages of seven and fourteen were presumed to be incapable of forming a criminal intent, but this presumption was rebuttable. Over the age of fourteen, children, like adults, were prima facie capable.

It was not uncommon for very young children to be prosecuted and punished. "Thus," says Blackstone, "a girl of thirteen has been burnt for killing her mistress; and one boy of ten, and another of nine years old, who had killed their companions, have been sentenced to death, and he of ten years actually hanged; because it appeared upon their trials, that the one hid himself, and the other hid the body he had killed, which hiding manifested a consciousness of guilt, and a discretion to discern between good and evil" (*Commentaries on the Laws of England* [1765], chap. 17).

who has committed an act that, if committed by an adult, would be a crime), a "person in need of supervision" (a child who has committed an act that, if committed by an adult, would not be a crime), a "dependent" (a child whose parent is unable to care for him), or a "neglected" child (a child whose parents are derelict in their duty to care for him). Finally, the child so adjudged does not appear before the court for "sentencing" but instead is subjected to a "dispositional hearing" in which the question is not what the court shall do *to* the child (what sort of punishment it shall mete out), but what the court can do *for* the child (what the rehabilitative options are).

Neglect and the Right to Welfare. In addition to the positive right to rehabilitation promised to the child offender by the juvenile court, there are a number of other positive rights presently possessed by children but generally denied to adults. First, the child has the right (under "neglect" statutes) to be provided with a proper home, subsistence, education, medical care, and a proper moral environment. The correlative duty bearers are his parents or other legally responsible custodians. This duty is enforced by placing the latter under the supervision of the court's probation service, taking the child temporarily out of the home into institutional care or a foster home while conditions are being remedied at home, or, in extreme cases, terminating the rights of the parent completely under the appropriate statute.[4]

Second, since 1912 in the United States, children have had certain positive rights to welfare services under federal law. At present children who qualify* have the right to: (1) supportive services in their own homes, such as mental health and family agency services, protective services, and case work service in the Aid to Families with Dependent Children (AFDC) program; (2) supplementary service such as day care, homemaker service, and income maintenance programs, principally AFDC; and (3) substitute care services such as foster family care, adoption, and institutional child care.[5]

These can be seen as services that enable the parent or guardian to provide the child with the minimum specified under the neglect statutes. However, we must be clear about the content of the rights specified in the statutes. Thus, to say that a child has the right to a "proper home" does not imply that the child has the right to the direct, full-time care of at least one of his parents. His parents, by choice or necessity, may work at a job outside

*A child qualifies when his family is needy, he has a relative living in the same house, and at least one parent cannot or does not support or care for him (42 U.S.C. Sec. 606[a]).

the home and arrange for substitute care. Nor does this right entail that the child can obtain from his parent a certain amount of care and attention (for example, the degree of affection that will insure healthy psychological growth). Again, the right to "subsistence" does not specify anything but the minimum for a child's nutritional needs; it does not imply, for example, that a child has the right to an early childhood nutritional program that will guarantee that he maximizes his potential physical and mental growth. Finally, the right to "medical care" only specifies that the child has the right to be treated for conditions that may cause death, disfigurement, or substantial impairment of bodily functions. It does not specify, for example, that the child is owed participation in *preventive* medical programs.

Negative Claim Rights

The Right Not to Be Abused. Children, like adults, have the negative claim right not to be physically harmed by others, but there is an important way in which this right is qualified for children. The qualification is that the law permits a parent, a guardian, or (in many states) a teacher to use physical force as a mode of discipline.* Hence, although it would be an assault for a parent or teacher to strike his neighbor, it may not be an assault for him to strike his child or student.

The amount of physical force that a parent or teacher can use is limited. Usually it must be "reasonable" or "not excessive." The problem, of course, is to settle on some standard of "reasonable force" so that a clear line can be drawn between discipline and child abuse. The existing state statutes present a number of definitional options. For example, one approach is to define abuse by specifically delineating the types of injury that justify intervention. Other statutes merely contain generalized references to children who have been "mistreated" or "physically abused."[6]

The incidence of child abuse has greatly increased in recent years.† One response that states have made to this is to pass statutes requiring doctors to report suspected child abuse, removing any possibility of liability for reporting, and facilitating admission into evidence of reporting doctors' testimony in court.[7] In many states schoolteachers, social workers, and all medical professionals (dentists, nurses, etc.) are required to report as well. In all cases, failure to report reasonable suspicions of child abuse is punishable as a misdemeanor.[8]

*The U.S. Supreme Court has recently ruled that corporal punishment in the schools is not unconstitutional (*Ingraham* v. *Wright*, 51 L. Ed. 2d 711, decided 19 April 1977).

†There are 2–4 million American children annually who are subjected to bodily injury.

Second, in addition to physical abuse, courts will also intervene when a child has been sexually abused. Again, there is no generally accepted definition of the term. It clearly includes intercourse, with or without force or threat, but whether it includes other forms of sexual contact is not clear. This is largely because it is "difficult to distinguish between appropriate displays of affection or fondling and other possibly disturbing activity."[9]

Privacy and Reputation. In addition to the right not to be abused, there are two other negative claims worthy of mention. First, a child, like an adult, has the right to an undamaged reputation. This right is secured by the fact that he or she may (has the power to) sue for defamation.[10] Second, a child, unlike an adult, has few privacy rights. However, one privacy problem that adults and children share is that both are the subject of many data collection systems. Examples of existing systems on children include: (1) local school system files, which typically include background identifying data, grades, a summary health record, scores on IQ tests, subjective evaluations by teachers, and several references to reported misconduct by the child; (2) local juvenile court files, which typically include the arrest record, the court record, results of psychological tests, a social history, and the disposition of the case of those children who have had contact with the juvenile justice system; and (3) government agency files, for example, the Office of Education of the Department of Health, Education and Welfare's data bank containing educational and medical data pertaining to the children of migrant workers. None of these collection systems as such constitutes an invasion of privacy. However, privacy is violated if, for example, there are no adequate safeguards established to assure the confidentiality of the information or to assure that risk of harm to the child from labeling or mislabeling him (such as "retarded," "delinquent," etc.) is outweighed by a governmental interest in collecting the information. With the exception of one significant case on the subject of data collection,[11] children do not as yet have the right to privacy in the sense specified.

The second aspect of privacy relevant to children is their susceptibility to search and seizure of their possessions at home and in school. Under the Fourth Amendment to the U.S. Constitution, children have the right to be free from illegal searches and seizures. However, since (1) the Fourth Amendment is not applicable to searches conducted by persons who are not government agents, and (2) the child's parent can consent to a police search of the child's room, then a child cannot claim a violation of his Fourth Amendment rights when his parent searches his room or when the police search his room after obtaining parental consent. Second, since a schoolteacher or administrator acts *in loco parentis* with respect to the child and is a private person, not an officer of government, his conduct is not subject to the Fourth Amendment. Thus, he has the right to conduct a warrantless search of a child's school locker and desk. However, the right to search is not unlimited: before he can search, he must at least have "reasonable suspicion" that something of an illegal nature is in the possession of the student.[12]

Liberties

The differences between children and adults with respect to their liberty and (mixed) liberty/power rights are as great as are the differences between them with respect to their positive and negative rights. In the latter case, as we have seen, children possess a greater number of such rights than do adults. In the case of liberty and liberty/power rights, to be discussed in this and the next section, the advantage clearly belongs to the adult: the number of such rights possessed by children is comparatively small.

At Home. Children are denied many of the liberty rights possessed by adults largely because of the nature of their legal relationship to their parents. Parents have certain legal rights and duties with respect to their children, and these rights and duties imply a lack of certain liberty rights in their children. For example, because of the fact that every child has a "guardian of his person," usually his natural parent, the parent and not the child has the right to choose the child's name, his religion, and the kind of education he is to receive. Second, because of the fact that the child has a "custodian" (again, this is usually his natural parent) who has duties to provide maintenance and supervision and to meet his general welfare needs, it is the parent, not the child, who has the right to decide where the child shall live, what he will eat, and how he will dress. Nor does the child have the right to his own earnings. The parent, as custodian, may claim them. Finally, the duty of a custodian to provide a favorable moral environment for the child probably implies a right to censor the books the child reads and the movies he sees. As one author has remarked, a list of categories such as this cannot begin to exhaust the universe of parental rights over a child and the corresponding lack of liberty rights in the latter. The scope of effective parental rights in a particular household "probably is restrained more by the imagination of the parents and the efficiency of the available sanctions than by law."[13] This has certainly not changed much since Roman and common law.*

In School. All children within certain age limits are subject to state statutes compelling their education. Compulsory education laws have uniformly been sustained against various charges that individual liberties guaranteed by the Constitution are unreasonably infringed. However, a basic constitutional limitation placed on these statutes by the Supreme Court is that attendance at public school is not the only way to satisfy the requirement. Thus, although children and their parents do not have the freedom to choose whether or not the children attend school, parents are free to choose between public and private school for their children,[14] or if they can convincingly show that their religious faith had so pervaded and regulated the whole mode of life of their children that it would be gravely endangered if not destroyed by enforcement of the requirement of compulsory formal education beyond the eighth grade, then the child may not be required to submit to such education.[15] However, since these are rights that the Supreme Court has granted to the *parents* of the child, not to the child, I should not designate these as liberty rights of children.

The doctrine of *in loco parentis* gives local school authorities the right to adopt reasonable regulations covering student conduct while in school. The

*Although the change has been for the better. In order to understand the extraordinary legal status of the child in Roman law it is necessary to introduce the conception of the paterfamilias, the head of the family. "His children, *of whatever age*, though they are citizens and therefore have rights in public law, are subject to his unfettered power of life and death" (Barry Nicholas, *An Introduction to Roman Law* [Oxford: Oxford University Press, 1962], p. 66). Indeed, in early Roman law the paterfamilias could dispose of his children as he wished. He could kill them or sell them as slaves.

At common law, the father did not have quite so much legal power over his children as that possessed by the Roman paterfamilias. His right to restrict his child's liberty lasted only until the child was twenty-one years of age, at which time the child acquired all adult legal rights. And although the father could give or bequeath away his child's custody, he could not kill him or sell him into slavery. However, it is not entirely clear whether it was his duty to maintain his offspring, that is, whether there was anything in common law that would prevent a father from simply refusing to supply his child with the food, clothing, and shelter required to guarantee his survival. Finally, although the father could not sell the child into permanent slavery, he could for a fee give custody to another for the remainder of the child's minority.

In England, "infant girls were sold to be raised as prostitutes, and boys to work" (Mary Van Stolk, *The Battered Child in Canada* [Toronto: McClelland and Steward, 1972], p. 103). Indeed, the system in both England and colonial America of "pauper apprenticeship" bears strong analogy to slavery. Under the system instituted in the time of Henry VIII, any child over the age of five years could be apprenticed in order to eliminate the poverty of the parent. In the American colonies, a Virginia law of 1646 ordered county commissioners to select poor children at least seven or eight years old and send them to Jamestown to work in the public flax houses (Harold Goldstein, "Child Labor in America's History," *Children Today* 5 [1976]: 30).

rationale of this is that the state has a compelling interest in the maintenance of a proper atmosphere for learning in its schools.[16] For example, a child in school may not have the (liberty) right to wear immodest or suggestive clothing, and many courts have permitted regulations on specific items of clothing (such as girl's jeans) and hair length for males. Again, state statutes and local school boards may restrict a student's right of association by regulating membership in secret societies, on the ground that such societies "can have a detrimental influence on the schools by tending to destroy good order, discipline, and scholarship."[17]

Children and their advocates have recently begun to gain some significant liberty rights on the ground that the regulations denying them these rights do not bear a reasonable relation to material and substantial disruption. Thus, a school cannot control a student's "symbolic expression" of a political point of view if the expression merely makes others uncomfortable.[18] Second, children within the age limits of statutorily permitted school attendance cannot be barred for reason of marriage, nor can they be isolated from contact with other students within the school setting or prevented from participating in extracurricular activities. Third, although school officials may enact student newspaper regulations that prohibit distribution of material that will cause interference with school operation and discipline, they may not restrain student publications in the absence of a reasonable prediction of disruption.

A question that frequently arises in the education area is whether a particular subject or activity can be required, that is, whether a student has the liberty right to choose not to take a course or participate in an activity. It would appear that the student has few such rights. Where there is a clash on this issue it is between the right of the state to require the study of subjects essential to good citizenship and the right of parents to guide the upbringing of their children. There is one notable exception. In 1943 the Supreme Court struck down a state regulation requiring that children salute the flag and pledge allegiance.[19] Although he is obviously subject to parental influence in such matters, my interpretation of this ruling is that the *child* has the liberty right to choose not to salute the flag and recite the pledge.

Finally, it should be noted that the above discussion is restricted to public schools. None of the liberty rights accorded the public school student are necessarily granted to the child attending private school.

Outside of Home and School. There are several ways in which the state restricts the liberty of children outside of home and school regardless of the wishes of the child or his parents. First, the right of a child to work is severely limited by both federal and state law, a reaction to the exploitative practices of the not too distant past.* The present laws and regulations governing child labor are a "complex mosaic of prohibitions and exemptions," but the following generalizations can be safely asserted:

> Under the federal law . . . 18 is the minimum age for employment in non-agricultural occupations declared hazardous, while 16 is the minimum age for general employment and for employment in hazardous occupations in agriculture. Fourteen- and 15-year olds may be employed outside school hours under certain hours limitations and in certain relatively safe occupations, except in manufacturing; and children of any age may be employed in non-hazardous occupations in agriculture outside of school hours. There are a limited number of exemptions from child labor standards in specific occupations under prescribed conditions. . . . Where state laws have different standards, the higher of the two standards applies.[20]

The second major area in which a child may feel legal restrictions on his freedom to act or not act as he chooses is that of curfew laws. Most states have laws that prevent children under sixteen—and in some instances under eighteen—from being in public places after a 10 or 11 p.m. curfew. At the state level, the judicial response to such laws has been inconsistent. However, in the first federal case of its kind, the constitutionality of a juvenile curfew ordinance was recently upheld.[21]

Third, it hardly needs to be pointed out that children are subject to the same restrictions of the criminal law that are imposed on adults. A child, like an adult, is not free to commit acts of murder, assault, fraud, or trespass. However, as indicated above, there are a number of acts that would not be criminal if committed by an adult but that cannot be committed by children. These include the following misdeeds: running away from home; being incorrigible, ungovernable, and beyond the control of parents; being truant; engaging in sexual relations; and becoming pregnant. This mixture of noncriminal acts is referred to by lawyers as "juvenile status offenses" since only persons of juvenile status are legally prohibited from doing them

*The industrial revolution in the latter half of the eighteenth century only served to increase dramatically the parental practice of binding out children to work in order to accumulate profit. This significant increase occurred largely because the division of labor into simple tasks and the use of power machinery made it feasible to employ cheap unskilled workers without much physical strength. Harold Goldstein notes that a visit to a typical spinning mill in Providence, Rhode Island, in 1800 "found all the work being done by children from four to 10 years of age, with one adult as superintendent. In 1820 about half of all textile workers in Massachusetts, Connecticut and Rhode Island were children, and in 1832 42 precent of cotton mill workers were boys under 12. A 12- or 14-hour work day was typical, and many children worked a night shift" ("Child Labor in America's History," *Children Today* 5 [1976]: 34). In many cases the children worked with irons riveted around their ankles to keep them from running away. They were beaten and starved, and many died as a result of occupational diseases. Some committed suicide (Mary Van Stolk, *The Battered Child in Canada* [Toronto: McClelland and Steward, 1972], p. 104).

and only such persons can be apprehended, be adjudicated (as a "person in need of supervision"), and, as a consequence, suffer a lengthy loss of liberty for committing them.

There are other liberty rights granted to adults but denied to children that deserve brief mention. Children do not have the liberty right to visit or remain in certain kinds of places (for instance, dancing halls or pool or billiard rooms), to drive an automobile or fly an airplane, to purchase or consume alcoholic beverages, or to purchase or obtain pornographic material.[22]

Finally, to end on an optimistic note, legislation in some states has granted to children the liberty right to obtain treatment or counseling for certain specified illnesses, conditions, or health purposes. "These laws, which usually contain either a very low age for consent or no age floor at all, typically have been extended to include one or more of such matters as venereal disease, drug addiction, or rehabilitation, pregnancy, childbirth, and family planning or birth control. Some also extend to any reportable disease."[23] More recently, the Supreme Court has ruled that it is unconstitutional for a state to exclude such a matter as terminating a pregnancy by abortion from the preceding list of liberty rights. A pregnant minor need not obtain the consent of a parent in order to terminate her pregnancy during the first twelve weeks.[24] Third, the Court ruled in 1977 that young people have a legal right (are at liberty) to purchase nonprescriptive contraceptives, thereby striking down legal barriers to such purchases that existed in about fifteen states.[25]

Mixed Rights: Liberties/Powers

Ideally, this section should confine itself exclusively to powers, but it is difficult to find any "pure" cases of powers to illustrate the contrast between the legal status of children and that of adults. Thus, a possible candidate for a power right that is denied to children is the right to marry. However, as noted in the preceding chapter, on closer inspection this is a mixed right: it combines a liberty right (if you have the right to marry then no one has a right that you not marry) and a power right (if you go through the prescribed ritual, you alter your marital status), and both the power and the liberty presuppose that the possessor has the standing, the capacity right, to marry. Hence, what I shall discuss in this section are those rights that are combinations of liberties and powers.

First, children lack the right to marry. Although the rules are complex and have a number of exceptions built into them, it is generally the case that a male minor cannot marry until the age of eighteen. A female minor, on the other hand, need only be sixteen years old to marry. Both males and females over the requisite age limit but still under the age of twenty-one must obtain parental consent in order to marry.

Second, most persons classified as children lack the right to vote in municipal, state, and federal elections. In most states a male or female child cannot vote until he or she has reached the age of eighteen years.

Third, a child does not have the right to execute a will for real or personal property. The minimum age for the execution of a will is twenty-one years in most states, although the age varies from state to state and in several states the minimum age required for executing a will for personal property has been lowered to eighteen years (in South Carolina a girl of twelve years of age may execute this kind of will).

Fourth, children do not have the right to make certain contracts. The law expresses this by calling such contracts "void." Thus, a child's written promise to be a surety on a bond is void, and he lacks the right to perform such an act, even with the consent of his guardian.

However, most of the contracts of children are "voidable," that is, the child has the liberty/power right to avoid the contract if he chooses. Some writers have misleadingly argued that this means that the child is "under both a legal and practical disability": the former in that he cannot give legal assurance that he will not disaffirm; the latter in that adults will frequently refuse to contract with or sell to children.[26] This interpretation seems to me to be in part mistaken. Although I readily concede that children labor under a "practical disability" because their contracts are voidable, there is no "legal disability." If there were a legal disability, then we should have to say that the child does not have the power to make contracts. But he does have this power. The proof of this is that the other party to the contract is bound by it. Hence, the fact that a child can disaffirm his contract does not entail that he is under a legal disability.

Fifth, it is often pointed out that children share at least one important liberty/power right with adults: the right to bring an action and to recover damages for torts inflicted upon them. A child may sue and recover not only against the person directly responsible for his injury but also against any person who may have contributed in any way to it. And yet even possession of this right diminishes considerably in importance when we recognize its single exception: in most states children do not have the right to sue their parents for negligent or injurious conduct.*

*A. J. Kleinfeld reports that in the past few years the courts have created numerous exceptions to the parental immunity rule, "as where the child is emancipated, serious personal injuries are inflicted, the parent is dead, or the injury is inflicted in the course of a business

Mixed Rights: Due Process

As noted in chapter 1, the phrase "right to due process" in fact refers to a mixture of different kinds of rights, all brought together here for the sake of covenience. There are two major areas in which children have been recent recipients of the right to due process of law: juvenile court adjudicatory hearings and school disciplinary hearings. In each case, however, it is to be noted that only *some* of the kinds of rights that are referred to as part of "due process" have been granted to children.

Juvenile Court Procedure. Although the avowed purpose of the juvenile court is rehabilitation of the child, the Supreme Court ruled in 1967 that the fact-finding or adjudicatory hearings of the juvenile court were to be measured by due process standards in all cases in which the child is in danger of loss of liberty because of commitment.[27] In such cases the child is to be accorded the due process rights to adequate, timely, written notice of the allegations against him, to counsel, to non–self-incrimination, and to confront and cross-examine opposing witnesses under oath. In 1970, the Court added to this group the right of a juvenile to a standard of proof beyond a reasonable doubt, at least in those delinquency proceedings "when a juvenile is charged with an act which would constitute a crime if committed by an adult."[28] However, in the following year it refused to hold that a juvenile is constitutionally entitled to the right of trial by jury.[29] Its reason for this ruling was partly that "due process" refers to the fact-finding processes of juvenile proceedings. "But one cannot say that in our legal system the jury is a necessary component of accurate fact-finding."[30]

School Disciplinary Hearings. In a recent case the U.S. Supreme Court set out the minimum constitutional requirements in cases involving suspensions of children from school of ten or fewer days. The Court said that due process requires that the student be given oral or written notice of the charges against him and, if he denies them, an explanation of the evidence the authorities have and an opportunity to present his side of the story. However, it further said that there need be no delay between the time notice is given and the time of the hearing. The Court expressly rejected requirements for allowing representation by counsel, for presenting witnesses, and for confronting and cross-examining adverse witnesses.

---

activity carried on by the parent as master with the child as a servant" ("The Balance of Power among Infants, Their Parents and the State, Part 2," *Family Law Quarterly* 5 [1972]: 427).

But it did say that longer suspensions or expulsions may require more formal procedures.[31]

Immunities

Hohfeld remarked that an immunity has a certain contrast to a power. To have an immunity is to be free from the legal power or control of another. To fail to have an immunity, that is, to be subject to the control of another, is to suffer from a *liability*. If this contrast is accepted, then the status of child confers significant liabilities as well as immunities.

Torts and Contracts. Perhaps the most important immunity that a child possesses has already been mentioned: if he commits an offense, he cannot be tried in a criminal court under the ordinary rules of the criminal law (unless he is over a certain age and his offense is relatively serious). However, the common law rule still prevails for the tort liability of a child: he may be liable for such torts as assault and battery, trespass to land, conversion, defamation, seduction, deceit, and negligence.* The exceptions to this denial of immunity are, first, that a child may escape liability because he is found to be of such "tender years" that he is incapable of forming the specific intent required, so that the tort (for instance, deceit or battery) has not been committed, and "the event is to be classed as an unavoidable accident."[32] Second, since a child can disaffirm his contracts, and where the wrong complained of consists merely in the nonperformance or improper performance of an agreement, "the plaintiff will not be permitted to recover merely by changing the form of action to one of tort."[33]

Termination of the Right to Be Cared For. The most significant liability a child possesses is that of having his (positive) right to be with and cared for by his parents canceled or terminated. This is simply the corollary of the legal process of terminating parental rights. It is an aspect that is all too frequently ignored in discussions of the latter procedure.

It is important to explain carefully why I refer to termination by the state of parental rights as implying a liability or lack of immunity in a child. The

*At common law a parent could also be made liable for the torts of his minor child by virtue of his relationship of principal to his child as agent, e.g., if he were to order the child to do an act injurious to another.

parental rights that the state terminates are in part liberties, for example, the liberty to choose the child's manner of education, place of residence, and so on. But at the same time, the parent is also released from his legal duties or obligations with respect to the child, such as to provide food, shelter, clothing, medical care—in short, all of those duties that constitute caring for the child. The significance of this is that when the state releases the parent from these duties via a termination-of-rights proceeding the child no longer has a correlative claim right that his parent do any of those positive acts of care in his behalf. The child, then, by virtue of parental rights-termination proceedings is *liable* to an action that removes his positive claim rights against the parent. In short, the child lacks an important immunity.

A child is liable to have his positive rights terminated with respect to his natural parents in a number of ways, two of which I want to focus on here: voluntary surrender of rights by the parent, and involuntary abrogation of rights of parent over child through court order.

A parent usually voluntarily surrenders his rights (and is released from his duties) with respect to his minor child under a statutory procedure. Statutes normally provide that the court may place the child so long as the parent's consent is voluntarily and intelligently given. Thus, many statutes require: (1) that the mother have casework counseling to help her arrive at a decision with respect to her child's care; (2) that the mother be advised by legal counsel, with counsel appointed for her if she cannot afford to retain one; and (3) that the mother, her lawyer, and the agency representative appear in person before a juvenile judge, who will inquire into the mother's understanding of the relinquishment and its implications.[34]

Although these statutes have the advantage of terminating rights prior to the parents' becoming involved in "a difficult and emotionally wrenching adoption proceeding in which they suddenly realize the seriousness of their past consent and, second, that such termination is not subject to attack in later adoption proceedings, nor may the consent ratified by the court be withdrawn,"[35] it is still the case that the statutes center on the parent. There is no mention of the needs of the child in voluntary termination proceedings, nor is it necessary for the court to acquire the consent of the child prior to terminating his relationship with his parent.

The other procedure for terminating parental rights is perhaps more familiar. Involuntary termination of parental rights has two principal bases: abandonment of the child by the parent and neglect of the child by the parent. When the conduct of the parent(s) indicates that they intend to abandon their children, then parental rights will be permanently dissolved by the court. In some states, statutes define abandonment with some specificity.

> In New York, for example, an abandoned child is one left by both parents, or by the parent or person having custody of the child, in destitute circumstances, or without proper food, shelter, or clothing, or one left without parental visits to the child, or payments for his support for at least six months, if done without good reason. . . . The necessary intent to abandon is presumed if any of the above facts or conditions is proved to exist.[36]

In other states, the definition of the term is left up to the court, although similar sorts of conduct have been found to amount to abandonment.

I have already discussed neglect in the section on positive rights. My focus there was on the relationship between neglect statutes and the right of the child to be provided with a proper home, subsistence, education, medical care, and a proper moral environment. If the correlative duty is not performed by the parents, then in extreme cases termination proceedings may be undertaken in accordance with the appropriate statute. A typical extreme case would be repeated physical abuse of the child. In other cases the courts are reluctant to sever parental ties permanently if there is any hope of building a stable family. The professed goal of the court is to advance "the best interests of the child." However, there seems to be little consistency of opinion on what constitutes a child's best interests. Where it is thought that it is in a child's best interests not to have his moral development jeopardized, courts have removed children from their homes for a variety of reasons, for example, because the mother "frequented taverns" or had men visit overnight; the parents of the child adhered to "extreme" religious practices or lived in a communal setting; the parent was a lesbian or a homosexual; or the mother had an illegitimate child.[37] In other cases, where the courts have announced that they will intervene only if there is serious, specifically defined harm being done to the child, the life style or moral standards of the parents do not play a significant role in deciding whether to terminate parental rights.

Summary

Children have a number of legal rights that are not granted to the (competent) adult. These include the *positive claim rights* to rehabilitation (when adjudicated "delinquent"), to a proper home, to subsistence, to medical care, to education, and to a proper moral environment. Second, the child possesses the *negative claim rights* to have others refrain from acts of physical and sexual abuse and to refrain from acts that would constitute damage to his reputation. Third, the child (but not the adult) has the *liberty/power right* to avoid many of his contracts.

However, the list of legal rights possessed by the competent adult but denied the child seems to be significantly longer than the preceding inventory. Thus, the child lacks the *negative claim rights* against his parents and teachers to refrain from acts of physical punishment and to refrain from privacy invasions that would be constitutionally impermissible if he were an adult. Children also lack a large number of *liberty rights* possessed by adults (such as to do certain kinds of work at certain hours, to choose one's own place of residence, to decide whether and how to educate oneself, etc.), several *liberty/power rights* (to marry, to vote, to make wills), and the important *immunity right* against the state not to have one's relationship with one's parent or legal guardian terminated.

The traditional explanation of these differences in treatment is that children have certain deficiencies—intellectual, physical, and moral—that require that they be saddled with special burdens and disabilities and pampered with special protections. However, in recent years children have been accorded a few rights that once were possessed solely by competent adults. Most of these have been granted by the Supreme Court in a series of decisions purporting to establish constitutional rights of children against state intervention. These include the right to symbolic expression of political opinion, to obtain an abortion, and to purchase nonprescriptive contraceptives, and certain due process rights. Whether these decisions represent a significant break with tradition is a question I take up in the next chapter.

3 The Child As a Person: Recent Supreme Court Decisions

In reflecting on the vast differences in treatment accorded children and adults under U.S. law, one is soon brought to inquire about the rationales that have persuaded legislators to distribute legal rights in these ways. What arguments have compelled them to grant certain legal rights to competent adults while withholding them from children (and visa versa)? This is an empirical question that might be easily answered if we had some record of the reasons given by each legislator for voting as he did on a particular law. Unfortunately, there are few such records. Although we sometimes know from newspaper accounts and other sources why a particular legislator voted as he did, we do not know if *his* reasons were the reasons persuading his colleagues to vote as they did. We are usually left to make more or less reasonable conjectures in each case.

However, there is one branch of government that does not disappoint us in the search for existing rationales of decisions that have been made about the rights of children. This is the judicial branch. The various court reporters give us a comprehensive account of the majority and minority decisions and the reasons for reaching these decisions in at least those cases that are believed to be sufficiently important for the purposes of reporting.

Accordingly, in this chapter I shall provide an account of some of the recent decisions on children's rights that have been reached by the United States Supreme Court. I do this not only for purposes of illustrating existing rationales, but to show that the Supreme Court makes certain important but unproved assumptions about the way in which the interests of children are to be weighed or balanced against those of the state, schools, and parents. Second, I show that the fact that the Court is making these normative assumptions in reaching decisions about the rights of children is obscured by the Court's oft-stated but highly misleading claim that "children are persons" and thus have the full range of constitutional rights. Third, I argue that the Court is still in the process of discovering a set of rational moral principles to guide it in considering cases involving issues of children's rights. Hence, there is as much a need for a normative theory of juvenile rights at the level of judicial decision making as there is at the legislative.

The First Amendment: Tinker *and* Ginsberg

A case that is often appealed to by those arguing for granting more rights to liberty to children is *Tinker* v. *Des Moines Independent Community School District*.[1] The facts of the case are simple. The petitioners, three school children, decided to publicize their objections to the hostilities in Vietnam and their support for a truce by wearing black armbands to school. The principals of the Des Moines schools became aware of the plan and adopted a policy that any student wearing an armband to school would be asked to remove it, and if he refused he would be suspended until he returned without the armband. The children were aware of the regulation, but went ahead and wore their armbands. They were all suspended from school until they would come back without their armbands.

The Supreme Court held the regulation of the school district unconstitutional. Justice Fortas, who delivered the opinion, argued, first, "that the wearing of an armband for the purpose of expressing certain views is the type of symbolic act that is within the Free Speech Clause of the First Amendment"; second, that First Amendment rights are available to teachers and students: "students in school as well as out of school are 'persons' under our Constitution. They are possessed of fundamental rights which the State must respect"; and third, that although the Court recognizes the "comprehensive authority of the State and of school officials . . . to prescribe and control conduct in the schools," they cannot prohibit a particular expression of opinion without a showing that engaging in the forbidden conduct would "materially and substantially interfere with the requirements of appropriate discipline in the operation of the school."[2]* Finally, in the instant case, Fortas held that there is no such showing.

*Mr. Fortas also cites *Meyer* v. *Nebraska*, 262 U.S. 396 (1922) and *Pierce* v. *Society of Sisters*, 268 U.S. 510 (1924), to support his argument that students and teachers do not shed their constitutional rights "at the schoolhouse gate." However, it is certainly arguable that the cases cited can be used to support a constitutional argument for extending a right to liberty to children. Instead, these cases seem to give support to the thesis that *teachers* have the right to

There is no mention of paternalism in the argument of the Court, and the school district did not attempt to support its case by arguing that it was protecting the petitioners from doing harm to themselves. However, in a concurring opinion Justice Stewart raises the possibility that the Court is here inconsistent given the fact that in the preceding term it had held that First Amendment rights of children are *not* coextensive with those of adults. The point is well taken. In *Ginsberg* v. *State of New York*[3] the Court considered the question of whether it was constitutionally impermissible for New York to accord minors under the age of seventeen a more restricted right than that assured adults to judge and determine for themselves what sex material they read and see. Their answer was that it was not, and in their argument the Court relied on a line of reasoning developed much earlier in the case of *Prince* v. *Commonwealth of Massachusetts*, where it had stipulated that "the power of the state to control the conduct of children reaches beyond the scope of authority over adults."[4] In *Ginsberg* the Court tells us how far beyond this scope of authority the state may go. First, the state may design laws restricting the liberty of children more severely than that of adults if this will support those who have the responsibility for children's well-being (parents, teachers) in the discharge of that responsibility. Second, the state may design laws restricting children's liberty if it can show that these laws will protect the children's welfare and will see that they are "safe-guarded from abuses" that might prevent their "growth into free and independent, well-developed men."

Justice Stewart's doubts momentarily aside, it might be argued that *Tinker* does not conflict with the reasoning in *Ginsberg*. There is no

---

teach certain subjects in school and *parents* have certain rights with respect to how they control the education of their children. Thus, in *Meyer* the Court struck down a Nebraska statute that made it unlawful to "teach any subject to any person in any language than the English language" (Laws 1919, c. 249). The Court argued that this unduly restricts the liberty of the plaintiff (a teacher of the German language) to teach and the liberty of the parents to engage him to teach their children. Both of these liberties are rights guaranteed by the Fourteenth Amendment. The Court does not discuss the corresponding right of the *child* to choose to be taught a foreign language. If we are to construe this as a genuine case asserting a child's right to liberty then it seems to me that this would be a necessary ingredient. At the most, the right guaranteed the child by the decision in *Meyer* is the positive right to be provided with instruction in a foreign language, if his parents so choose.

We reach the same result in examining *Pierce*. In this case, the Court held unconstitutional the Oregon Compulsory Education Act of 1922, which required all normal children between the ages of eight and sixteen years to attend public school. This was held a violation of the Fourteenth Amendment in that the act "unreasonably interferes with the liberty of parents and guardians to direct the upbringing and education of children under their control" (573). No mention is made of the right of a child to choose to attend a public or private school. Instead, the only concern of the Court with children is to stress the judgment that in a conflict between their parents and the state over the general question of who should "nurture and direct [their] destiny," the parents should prevail.

plausible reason for thinking that school children would be "safeguarded from abuses" that would prevent them from growing into "free and independent, well-developed men" by the school board's policy preventing them from wearing armbands. That is, *Tinker* does not represent an abandonment by the Court of the paternalism it had applied in *Ginsberg*: there was simply no occasion to apply it in this case.

The conflict that undoubtedly troubled Justice Stewart was instead over a point that he had developed in his concurring opinion in *Ginsberg*. He had argued there that although the Constitution guarantees a society of free choice, "such a society presupposes the capacity of its members to choose":

> When expression occurs in a setting where the capacity to make a choice is absent, government regulation of that expression may co-exist with and even implement First Amendment guarantees. . . .
>
> I think a State may permissibly determine that, at least in some precisely delineated areas, a child—like someone in a captive audience—is not possessed of that full capacity for individual choice which is the presupposition of First Amendment guarantees. It is only upon such a premise, I should suppose, that a State may deprive children of other rights—the right to marry, for example, or the right to vote—deprivations that would be constitutionally intolerable for adults.[5]

It is not difficult to understand Justice Stewart's misgivings about concurring with the majority in *Tinker*. If children do not have adequate capacity to make the sort of choice relevant to reading certain magazines, then they surely cannot be said to have the capacity needed to choose whether or not symbolically to express a political opinion.

And yet one is left wondering what Stewart meant by "full capacity for individual choice." Under what conditions does someone lack it? A three-year-old child can choose between a red ball and a green ball; thus, in one sense of "capacity to choose," he can be said to have this capacity. But this is clearly not what Stewart means. Given his examples, I suspect that what he means is that children do not have the capacity to make *rational* choices in a certain range of situations, for example, marriage and voting. If this is so, then although one sort of problem is avoided, Stewart runs directly into another. Thus, one wants the answer to such questions as What is meant by the phrase "rational choice"? What empirical evidence is there to support the claim that children generally lack the ability to make rational choices (in the relevant cases)? Why is it important anyway to decide whether a class of beings possesses the ability to make rational choices before deciding whether to grant or deny that being or class a particular legal right?

This is not to disagree with Stewart's contention that there is a problem in reconciling the decision in *Tinker* with those in *Ginsberg* and *Prince*.

However, I think that the problem has a different source from that described by Stewart. In *Tinker* a child is declared to be a "person" and (therefore) a possessor of "fundamental rights which the State must respect." In other words, the *Tinker* court has declared that since children are to be included under the category of "persons" for constitutional purposes, then they are similar to adults at least in the respect that they too possess "fundamental rights." If this declaration had been used in *Ginsberg*, that decision might have been quite different. If children have fundamental rights, then they cannot be denied the exercise of these rights on grounds that could not be used in the case of an adult. In particular, a child, possessing First Amendment rights, could not be denied access to books or films on the ground that reading or viewing them would prevent her or his growth into a "free and independent, well-developed" individual. It is at least incumbent upon the Court to explain how children can possess fundamental rights and yet be justifiably denied the exercise of these rights. In what sense of "possess" do children possess First Amendment rights if it is possible to justify a decision to prevent them from reading or viewing the material they choose to read or view on grounds that would never be given justificatory weight in the case of adults? The *Tinker* court does not address this question.

The Right of Privacy: Danforth *and* Carey

The Supreme Court continued to place emphasis on the theme that children are persons and possess constitutional rights in two recent cases involving the right of privacy. In *Planned Parenthood of Central Missouri* v. *Danforth*,[6] the Court declared unconstitutional part of a Missouri abortion statute requiring an unmarried minor female to acquire the consent of her parent(s) or guardian(s) in order to have an abortion performed (unless the abortion is certified by a physician as necessary to preserve her life). Justice Blackmun, delivering the majority opinion, held that "constitutional rights do not mature and come into being magically only when one attains the state-defined age of majority. Minors, as well as adults, are protected by the Constitution and possess constitutional rights." In this case the relevant right is the "right of personal privacy, or a guarantee of certain areas or zones of privacy . . . [that] encompass a woman's decision whether or not to terminate her pregnancy." Blackmun conceded that although the Court "long has recognized that the State has somewhat broader authority to regulate the activities of children than of adults," upon examining whether there is any "significant state interest" in conditioning an abortion on the consent of a parent, he found that there is none. Parental interest in the termination of a child's pregnancy "is no more weighty than the right of privacy of the competent minor mature enough to have become pregnant."[7]

Second, the right of privacy was again invoked in *Carey* v. *Population Services International*.[8] In this case, which reached the Supreme Court in 1977, the Court overturned a New York law prohibiting the distribution of nonprescriptive contraceptives to minors under the age of sixteen years. Justice Brennan, writing for the majority, declared that "in a field that by definition concerns the most intimate of human activities and relationships, decisions whether to accomplish or to prevent conception are among the most private and sensitive." The Court rejected the attorney general's argument that the state had a legitimate interest in protecting morality by doubting whether limiting minors' access to contraceptives substantially discourages early sexual behavior. Moreover, the Court concluded, "It would be plainly unreasonable to assume that the state has prescribed pregnancy and the birth of an unwanted child or the physical and psychological dangers of an abortion as punishment for fornication."

Carey did not leave much room for a clash between constitutional rights and "legitimate state interests." Only one justice (Rehnquist) argued that the state had a legitimate interest to promote (deterring sexual activity among minors). However, there was a much stronger basis for dissent in *Danforth*. Several justices argued that there was one significant interest not considered by the majority that deserves serious consideration. The interest is the same as that cited in *Ginsberg*: the child's own welfare. Thus, Justice White protested that:

> Missouri is entitled to protect the minor unmarried woman from making the (abortion) decision in a way which is not in her own best interests, and it seeks to achieve this goal by requiring parental consultation and consent. This is the traditional way by which States have sought to protect children from their own immature and improvident decision; and there is absolutely no reason expressed by the majority why the State may not utilize that method here.[9]

In other remarks, Justice White refers us to the dissenting statement of his colleague Justice Stevens, who advances the strongest argument for the justification of paternalistic interferences with the liberty of the child:

> The State's interest in the welfare of its young citizens justifies a variety of protective measures. Because he may not foresee the consequences of his decision, a minor may not make an enforceable bargain. He may not lawfully work or travel as he pleases, or even attend exhibitions of constitutionally protected adult motion pictures. . . . The State's interest in protecting a young

> person from harm justifies the imposition of restraints on his or her freedom even though comparable restraints on adults would be constitutionally impermissible.[10]

My concern about the remarks of Stevens and White is similar to that expressed in my response to the difficulty of reconciling the decision in *Tinker* with that in *Ginsberg*. If it is an unconstitutional abridgment of the privacy right of an adult female to prohibit her from acquiring an abortion on the grounds that this is necessary to protect her from harm, then *once it is granted* that a minor female also has a constitutional right of privacy we cannot consistently prohibit her from acquiring an abortion on paternalistic grounds. In the seminal 1973 case of *Roe* v. *Wade*, the Supreme Court ruled that the decision to abort one's pregnancy comes within the scope of the constitutional right of privacy. But once having pronounced abortion to be within the area of constitutional protection, it is no longer open to the Court to "weigh" that protection against other considerations (for example, strengthening the family unit or protecting the female from harm). The Constitution says that its guaranteed rights, once correctly determined, "always have more weight than any possible combination of opposing interests, private or public."[11] If the Court proclaims that a child has the right of privacy, it cannot "weigh" or "balance" this right against family or other interests any more than it can do this in the case of the adult female. I would argue, then, that the real focus of the debate among Stevens, White, and the Court majority is not over the question whether in the case of children the right of privacy is to be outweighed by the state's interest in protecting them from harm (this makes no sense), but over the question whether children ought to be granted the constitutional right of privacy *at all*. It is only to the latter question that it is relevant to bring to bear considerations about state paternalism. The Court is barred from raising the issue of the child's welfare if it has already granted that children, like adults, *have* the right of privacy.

The Right to Due Process: In re Gault

The Supreme Court has decided five cases dealing in some way or other with procedure in the juvenile court. The most important of these decisions was in the case of *In re Gault*.[12] Put simply, the Court held that fact-finding (adjudicatory) hearings in the juvenile court "must measure up to the essentials of due process and fair treatment." This means that juveniles, in all cases, must be given adequate, timely, written notice of the allegations against them and, in cases in which they are in danger of losing their liberty because of commitment, they are to be accorded the right to counsel, to non–self-incrimination, and to confront and cross-examine opposing witnesses under oath.

Beginning with the assertion that "neither the Fourteenth Amendment nor the Bill of Rights is for adults alone," Justice Fortas (speaking for the majority) critically examined the following argument for the proposition that juveniles should *not* be accorded due process rights:

(1a) One can only obtain due process rights in criminal proceedings.

(1b) A juvenile court adjudicatory hearing is not a criminal proceeding. Therefore,

(1c) There is no obligation to accord due process rights to juveniles in juvenile court adjudicatory hearings.

The crucial premise in the preceding argument is statement (1a). Fortas's counter to that claim was to assert that the functional dividing line for the purpose of the due process clause of the Fourteenth Amendment is whether the proceeding may or may not result in loss of liberty, not whether the proceeding is criminal or civil, resulting in confinement to a jail or an institution with a benign-sounding name.

> A boy is charged with misconduct. The boy is committed to an institution where he may be restrained of liberty for years. It is of no constitutional consequence—and of limited practical meaning—that the institution to which he is committed is called an Industrial School. The fact of the matter is that, however euphemistic the title, a "receiving home" or an "industrial school" for juveniles is an institution of confinement in which the child is incarcerated for a greater or lesser time. His world becomes "a building with white-washed walls, regimented routine and institutional laws. . . ." Instead of mother and father and sisters and brothers and friends and classmates, his world is peopled by guards, custodians, state employees, and "delinquents" confined with him for anything from waywardness to rape and homicide.
>
> In view of this, it would be extraordinary if our Constitution did not require the procedural regularity and the exercise of care implied in the phrase "due process." Under our Constitution, the condition of being a boy does not justify a kangaroo court.[13]

In dissent, Justice Stewart ignored the fact that a juvenile proceeding may result in a loss of liberty for the child. What is important, he argued, is that the object of the proceeding is "correction of a condition," not "conviction and punishment for a criminal act." Given this object, a juvenile proceeding is not adversary, and the requirements of due process "have no inevitable place" in them. Indeed, to impose such requirements "is to invite a long step backwards into the Nineteenth Century" when children were tried in conventional criminal courts with all the conventions of criminal trials and were punished in much the same manner as adults.[14]

Although we may doubt that imposition of due process standards in the juvenile court will bring a return to the sort of response accorded the juvenile offender in the nineteenth century, one can sympathize with Stewart's claim that where the purpose of the juvenile court is therapy or rehabilitation of the child, the adversary system is ill suited to the task. Fortas meets this point, however, by arguing that *in fact* the juvenile court has failed in its rehabilitative purpose. Quoting his own words in a case decided one year earlier, Fortas observed that "there is evidence . . . that there may be grounds for concern that the child receives the worst of both worlds: that he gets neither the protection accorded to adults nor the solicitous care and regenerative treatment postulated for children."[15]

Part of the evidence that the goal of rehabilitation is not being achieved is the high recidivism rate among adjudicated delinquents. It is estimated that 60 percent of the children appearing in juvenile courts will return another time. Second, there is a great deal of doubt that any real effort can be made by the juvenile court judge to diagnose the causes and prescribe the cure for the individual child. Like the criminal courts, "juvenile courts are enormously overcrowded. Juveniles typically wait for hours for an informal hearing that may take only a few minutes. A juvenile court judge may adjudicate as many as ten or twenty cases a day; assembly line rather than individualized justice is the norm."[16] Coupled with the low level of training in law and the social sciences, clearly inadequate to make diagnoses, predictions, and prescriptions for each offender, it is not surprising that the juvenile court judge cannot and does not provide "individualized" attention to those who appear before him. In sum, since juveniles get the worst of one world, namely, confinement without the promised solicitous care and regenerative treatment, the Court has decided in *Gault* that the Constitution demands that they be relieved of the burden of the other world and granted some of the due process protections accorded adults in the criminal courtroom.

Conclusion

The rhetorical question posed at the outset of this chapter was whether the application by the Supreme Court of constitutional norms to individual children's rights cases will yield some generalizations. I believe that there are some general principles at work, but it seems clear that large questions about social policy remain, questions that cannot be answered by taking a harder look at the Constitution.

Consider, to begin with, the decisions reached by the Court in applying the First Amendment rights and the right of privacy to cases involving children. It will simply not do to attempt to sum up these cases with the remark that the Court, having decided that children are "persons," now sees them as possessed of the full range of constitutional rights. If the Court does see children as persons, then it surely sees them as a peculiar sort of person for purposes of constitutional analysis. They are persons who must be "safeguarded from abuses," and the state may continue to design laws that will help parents and teachers discharge their joint responsibility for these persons' well-being; since they do not have the "full capacity for individual choice," they may be deprived of certain rights (such as to marry or to vote), and their activities can be regulated if it can be shown (as it was not shown in *Danforth*) that this will "safeguard the family unit and parental authority." In short, the catch phrase that children are persons is precisely that: a phrase that lacks the precision of a normative principle. Although we learn from it that children have *some* legal rights under the Constitution (and thus are in a different category from animals or trees), since the Court obviously does not intend by it that children have equal rights with adults, we are left without a principle to inform us about *which* constitutional rights ought to be extended to children.

In my discussion of *Danforth* I suggested that the Court sometimes obscures the issue before it by implying that the debate about children's rights is over the question of whether a child's acknowledged constitutional rights are to be outweighed by the State's interest in protecting her or him from harm. I argued that this way of phrasing the question makes little sense. The force of saying that a person has a "constitutional right" to do something is that no court may "weigh" that protection against such considerations.[17]* For example, to say that an American citizen has the right to express in speech or writing his opinion that a policy of his government is unwise, unjust, or otherwise mistaken is to refer to a right that

*This does not mean that a constitutional right is "absolute" in the sense that its scope is unlimited: "the scope of free speech must necessarily be narrower than the range of all possible speech." However, it does mean that once the boundaries of a constitutional right's domain have become reasonably clear and stable it will be unconditionally obligatory within that domain. "The courts would decide whether a given exercise of free speech, for example, falls *clearly* within the boundaries of First Amendment protection; if it does, then any statute that prohibits it, or any governmental action that restricts it, must be declared unconstitutional" (Joel Feinberg, *Social Philosophy* [Englewood Cliffs, N.J.: Prentice-Hall, 1973], p. 81). Such rights are absolute, then, in the sense of laying *unconditionally incumbent* duties of respect and enforcement upon the courts.

is universally accepted as absolutely unconditional in its central core cases. The guarantee expressed in the First Amendment is not subject to judicial overruling as a result of "interest balancing" in a given case. Hence, if a child is said to have First Amendment rights, then it is never open to a legislative body to deny him or her access to certain sorts of reading matter on grounds that it would not use in the case of an adult.

The appropriate question for the Court to ask, then, is which constitutional rights ought to be extended to children. It is only in answering this question, I suggest, that it is relevant to weigh and balance the interests of the state, the child, and the parent. And viewed in this light, the Court does indeed seem to be in a quandary. There is the desire to accord certain First Amendment rights to children (because they are "persons"), yet there is a strong pull in the direction of denying them these rights on the dual ground that children should be protected from the consequences of their own "improvident and immature" decisions and that the authority of a parent or guardian in supervising a child's upbringing ought to be given state support. As a result, we are left with normative problems about which the Constitution gives no guidance: "What moral liberty-rights, if any, do children have, *qua* persons?" "Is it permissible legally to deny children the exercise of these rights if this is necessary to promote the child's own good?"

The due process cases also illustrate the point that the Court, despite its own assertions, views children as a different class of person and that, because of their differences from adults, they ought to be treated differently. Indeed, if the Court did not think this, then it would be hard pressed to find a justification for the practice of responding to juvenile offenders with a system of rehabilitation and therapy rather than punishment. Thus, the opinion in *Gault* sees nothing improper in the early conception of the juvenile court in which "a fatherly judge touched the heart and conscience of the erring youth by talking over his problems, by paternal advice and admonition, and in which, in extreme situations, benevolent and wise institutions of the State provided guidance and help 'to save him from a downward career.' " The implication of this is that if reality had matched the rhetoric, if the rehabilitative promise of the juvenile court had been kept, *Gault* would never have been decided. The policy question this presents is one that is never reached by the *Gault* court: is there an adequate justification for treating juvenile offenders separately through a system of specialized courts whose goal is to rehabilitate the child? If the child is a "person" under the Constitution and/or if the juvenile court system does not keep its promise of therapy, moral education, and rehabilitation, then one wonders what the justification is for treating the juvenile offender differently from the adult criminal. On the other hand, if the child is fundamentally different from the adult, and/or if the rehabilitative promise of the juvenile court is kept, then there may after all be ample ground for reexamining the requirement that standards of due process be applied in the juvenile court setting.

To repeat: none of the preceding questions is going to be answered by further analysis of the Constitution or past decisions of the Supreme Court. They each involve questions of social policy. Such questions can only be settled by attempting to formulate normative principles, in brief, to construct a general theory of juvenile rights. To this task I now turn.

Part 2

Toward a Theory of Juvenile Rights

4 Two Arguments from Moral Agency

My object in this part of the book is critically to examine a number of arguments that have been or that might be used to justify the common practice of denying certain legal rights to children while granting them others. Although I find none of these arguments persuasive, several contain elements that are necessary for the construction of what I will contend in part 3 to be the correct theoretical basis for deciding what legal rights children ought to possess. Hence, my purpose in these chapters is not entirely destructive. Indeed, if I make any contribution in this area it is only because the groundwork has been so well laid by ethical theorists who, though they may not have thought explicitly about the legal status of children, have argued for basic moral principles to which one must attend in constructing a normative theory of legal rights.

In the interest of avoiding troublesome ambiguity, I adopt the following definitions. First, unless otherwise indicated, I use the word "child" as it is presently used in the law, that is, to refer to a person under the age of eighteen years (the "age of majority" in most states). Second, when the word "parent" is used it is meant to include guardians and others who act in the place of parents. Third, the word "adult" is used to refer to someone over eighteen years and "competent adult" refers to an adult who is not legally declared incompetent (that is, who does not have the legal status of one who is "unable to manage his own affairs"[1]). Finally, and of most importance for what follows, I introduce two technical terms. I use the term "legal A-liberties" to refer to those legal liberties and liberty/power rights that are commonly granted (at present) to competent adults but not to children. The term "legal C-claims" will be used to refer to those legal, positive claim rights that are commonly granted (at present) to children but not to adults. Examples of legal A-liberties and legal C-claims are to be found in chapter 2.

The question that I pose for discussion in this and the next three chapters is this: is there a sound argument for either the proposition that the state is justified in denying legal A-liberties to children or the proposition that the state is justified in granting children legal C-claims or both? I consider five arguments that have been or might be used to prove either or both of these propositions: two versions of the argument from moral agency, the argument from the social contract, the argument from beneficence, and the argument from utility. The first three employ a deontological principle as central to their argument; the last two employ a teleological principle.[2] However, for methodological reasons that should become obvious as I proceed, I discuss these arguments in the following order: the two arguments from moral agency are considered in this chapter, the arguments from beneficence and utility are discussed in chapters 5 and 6, respectively, and the argument from the social contract is discussed in chapter 7.

Two final comments before proceeding. First, I do not consider all of the arguments that have been given for denying legal A-liberties or granting legal C-claims to children.*[3] Space limitations dictate that I restrict myself to those arguments that I find most plausible. Second, those who wish to argue that children should have precisely the same legal status that the state accords the competent adult might use two sorts of argument: *refutations* of arguments given in support of the propositions that the state is justified in denying legal A-liberties and granting legal C-claims to children and *positive* arguments designed to show that children ought to be given the same legal status accorded the competent adult. Although there are approaches to the topic of children's rights that have pursued the latter course,† by far the most popular tactic is the former. Again, largely because

*For example, I omit arguments employing the claim that children are mere chattel.

†Some liberationists have drawn on the observation of the historian Philippe Ariès that the idea of childhood is a European invention of the sixteenth century (*Centuries of Childhood: A Social History of Family Life*, trans. Robert Baldick [New York: Vintage, 1962], pp. 128 ff.). What Aries meant by this is that prior to the seventeenth century children were thought of as miniature adults. After this century and during the changes in our civilization wrought by the Reformation and the Renaissance the idea of a child as a unique being, different from an adult, began to flourish. The central component of this new idea was that children were "innocent," that as "fragile children of God" they did not have knowledge (experience) of good and evil. Hence, children were to be protected from exposure to adult ways (particularly to adult sexuality), and their freedom to engage in "adult" behavior was severely restricted so as to limit their opportunities to experience evil. Moreover, childhood was seen as a period in which

of space limitations, I restrict myself here to a consideration of those arguments that might be used to justify the denial of legal A-liberties or the granting of legal C-claims to children.

---

children must be prepared for adult life, that is, they are to be educated for the tasks of this distinctly different stage of their life by attending to the development of their character and reason.

Richard Farson has concluded from Aries's observations that since the idea of childhood does not describe a "natural state" of children, then societies are to be judged as more or less "normal" depending on how deeply the "myth of childhood" has become entrenched in their social fabric and in their laws. In more normal societies, he claims, children are treated the same as adults, at least in the sense that they have the same rights to liberty, and our society should approximate to this ideal (*Birthrights: A Bill of Rights for Children* [New York: Macmillan Co., 1974], p. 18).

The trouble with Farson's argument is that the premise does not entail the conclusion. Let us suppose that the claim that it is natural for children to be treated by adults no differently from the way they would treat other adults merely means that historically (i.e., prior to the seventeenth century) children were so treated. If this is a plausible interpretation (it is surely all that Aries intended to assert), then it does not entail the conclusion that we *ought* to treat children no differently from adults. In order to assert the latter claim we must at least adopt some other premise, such as that children would be happier if granted equal treatment. Unless such claims are advanced and supported by evidence, Farson's argument, standing on the single premise about the historical treatment of children, is invalid.

A more plausible "positive" argument for granting adult rights to children is found in Herbert Spencer's *Social Statics*, published several years before John Stuart Mill's famous essay *On Liberty*. In his argument (part of which is quoted in the epigraphs to this book), Spencer claimed that children, like adults, have the God-willed right to happiness: "happiness is attainable only through the medium of the faculties; for the production of happiness those faculties must be exercised; the exercise of them presupposes liberty of action; these are the steps by which we find our way from the Divine will to the law of equal freedom." He then claims that "the demonstration is fully as complete when used on behalf of the child as when used on behalf of the man." Finally, in answer to the objection that children do not have the cognitive capacity of adults, Spencer gives the following reply:

> The fullest endowment of rights that any being can possess is *perfect* freedom to exercise *all* his faculties. And if each of two beings possesses *perfect* freedom to exercise *all* his faculties, each possesses *complete* rights; that is, the rights of the two are *equal;* no matter whether their faculties are equal or not. For, to say that the rights of the one are less than those of the other, because his faculties are fewer is to say that he has no right to exercise the faculties he has not got!—a curious compound of truism and absurdity.

There are several questions one might have about this argument, but let me mention here only two difficulties that I find in it. First, the fact that one has the capacity to achieve happiness does not entail the conclusion that one ought to be granted "perfect freedom" to achieve that happiness (suppose, for example, that one is a sadist and thus achieves happiness by causing pain to others). Second, Spencer seems to ignore or be unaware of the various reasons for bringing in the observation that children do not have the cognitive capacity of an adult. Thus, as will be discussed in chapter 5, one might wish to argue that, lacking a certain degree of the capacity to reason and deliberate, children would be at great risk of doing harm to themselves if given perfect freedom of action. That is, although Spencer correctly observes that the fact that a child has less capacity to reason than an adult does not of itself entail the conclusion that children ought not to be permitted to do whatever they want to do to achieve happiness, those who point to this difference between children and adults never claim that it does! Instead, they use it to establish an independent claim in the course of their argument.

The Argument from "Actual" Moral Agency

The first of two arguments that I consider in this chapter I call the argument from "actual" moral agency. It is an argument that has firm roots in the history of social thought about the status of children—roots that get their philosophical sustenance from the works of Immanuel Kant[4] and John Locke.[5] The central idea is that of a "moral agent" or a "person." Such beings are said to have unique characteristics that are particularly relevant to the ascription of rights: the ability to be self-determining and the ability to be self-legislating. In the former case, the (self-determining) agent is able both to formulate purposes, plans, and policies of his own and to carry out these decisions, plans, or policies without undue reliance on the help of others. In the latter case, the (self-legislating) agent is able to adopt rules that he holds to be binding on himself and all rational beings.

The term coined by Kant to describe the capacity of a moral agent to be self-determining is *rational will.* A human being who possesses both this and the ability to be self-legislating has what Kant refers to as "autonomy of will." It was Kant's thesis that moral agents or persons "are not only self-determining but also formulate and follow rules, some of which (such as moral rules) they hold to be binding on others besides themselves."[6] That is, moral agents uniquely possess an autonomous will.

The second aspect of the argument from moral agency is the claim that moral agency (possession of an autonomous will) is a necessary condition for the ascription of certain moral rights. These were articulated by Locke as the right(s) not to be harmed (by others) in one's "life, health, liberty, or possessions."[7] This list is *negative*, that is, it imposes duties on others to refrain from interfering with the right holder in the specified ways. These are also *natural* rights, for moral agents possess them simply because they are moral agents, and quite independently of their varying social circumstances and degrees of merit. Third, they are *inalienable* rights, that is, they cannot be relinquished, transferred, or forfeited. Finally, it is only a moral agent to whom we are to ascribe these rights, for they are appropriate only for moral agents and not for any other animals or human beings. It is only by having these rights that the special status of moral agents can be protected and respected—their status as beings who make their own plans and execute them.

Kant would refer to the Lockean duties not to harm others in their life, health, liberty, or possessions as "perfect duties," for others are in a position to demand by *right* that they be complied with. However, the *basic* duty from which all others derive is expressed by Kant in the second formulation of the Categorical Imperative: "Act so that you treat humanity, whether in your own person or in that of another, always as an end and never as a means only."[8] If we translate this imperative into the language of rights, we can say that persons (moral agents) have the right to be treated as ends, meaning to be treated as beings having intrinsic value in themselves regardless of whatever value they may have or lack as a means to some end, and moral agents have the right not to be treated as things that are mere means. Thus, a farmer may treat both his plow and his hired hands as means, but although it is not a violation of a moral right to treat the plow merely as means, he would violate a moral right if he were to treat the hired hands in this way. Each hired hand, *qua* moral agent, is an end in himself and has the right to be treated that way, and he has the right precisely because he has an autonomous will.[9]

This also shows why it would be morally wrong for the state to behave paternalistically toward moral agents. Thus, if the state were to make it illegal for adults to smoke cigarettes on the sole ground that smoking may be dangerous to the health of the smoker, this would be an impermissible use of state coercion. It would violate the right of all persons to make their own choices to determine what happens to their life, and so would fail to treat them as ends in themselves.

How do these considerations apply to the case of children? Kant does not explicitly address the topic, but it is possible to make some reasonable conjectures about what he or a "Kantian" ethical theorist would say. First, it seems clear that the preceding considerations could not be used to support the proposition that the state would be justified in granting legal C-claims to children. A Kantian would not deny that we have moral duties to protect and provide for children. However, he would argue that they are not perfect duties, for neither children nor anyone else (including moral agents) can demand by right that we perform these positive acts. Moreover, the duty to protect and provide for children must be a perfect duty if it is to be justifiable for the state to enforce it by granting legal C-claims to children. In other words, Kant confines the sphere of legally enforceable duties to perfect duties to others. Jeffrie Murphy puts Kant's point in this way: "Law is justified only to the extent that it preserves the freedom of all beings affected by it. Legal coercion is justified only to secure freedom. Only if I unjustly limit another man's freedom is the State justified in restraining me through the coercive machinery of its force."[10] The adults or children who are simply unhappy have no claim against me if I fail to protect or provide for them. I have not violated their freedom; I have merely exercised my right to leave them alone. It is for this reason, then, that Kant confines the sphere of legally enforceable rights to the perfect duties mentioned above, and it is for this reason that his arguments could not be used to justify granting legal C-claims to children.

However, Kantian considerations can be brought to bear to support the proposition that the state is justified in denying legal A-liberties to children. The argument is short. Since children do not possess an autonomous will, they are not moral agents and thus have none of the natural rights listed above. Hence, it is justifiable for the state to deny legal A-liberties to children, for in doing so the state does not violate any (perfect) duties toward children, for example, to treat them as ends in themselves. Since children lack the natural right to be treated as ends (they are not moral agents), they have no right to make those choices that will determine what happens to their own lives, and the state has no duty to respect those choices that children should happen to make.

Discussion of the Argument

Although lists of human or natural rights drawn in the last half-century invariably include positive claim rights, I am going to restrict the list to be used in the argument from "actual" moral agency to Locke's negative claim rights. For the sake of convenience I shall call this group "natural N-rights." The Kantian argument for the proposition that the state is justified in denying legal A-liberties to children refers only to natural N-rights. It has the following simple structure:

(1a) If a being has natural N-rights, then he or she is a moral agent.

(1b) Children are not moral agents.

Therefore,

(1c) Children do not have natural N-rights.

(1d) If a being does not have natural N-rights, then it is justifiable for the state to deny this being legal rights.

Therefore,

(1e) It is justifiable for the state to deny legal A-liberties to children.

Each premise of the argument demands at least brief attention. I will discuss them all in reverse order, reserving most of my attention for premise (1a).

Natural and Legal Rights. Premise (1d) makes the dubious claim that lack of (all) the natural rights in Locke's list is a sufficient condition for the justified denial of legal A-liberties. But suppose, for the sake of argument, that children are beings who have no natural N-rights. Even so, we would not think that this is a sufficient reason for refusing to grant them certain legal rights, for we might think that there are other considerations that should be given equal weight. For example, it might be argued that if the state were to deny children the legal right not to be abused by their parents, this would have certain undesirable consequences. In addition to the increase in pain suffered by children, it would have bad effects on those who love and care for children (grief and other possible psychological damage), it would encourage others to take child abuse less seriously than they do now, and it might undermine the reluctance of some parents to be cruel to their children. In short, the question of whether a legal right should be granted to a class of beings is not entirely settled by deciding whether members of that class do or do not have natural N-rights.

Moral Agents and Children. The concept of a moral agent used in premise (1b) specifies a being who is able to carry out plans of his own devising (a being who is self-determining) and a being who can engage in the higher order activity of conceiving of and adopting rules for himself (a being who is self-legislating). My question is whether premise (1b) is true, that is, is it the case that children are not moral agents (in the sense specified)?

Professor Francis Schrag has recently argued that there is *no* criterion that dramatically distinguishes older from younger human beings. He states that he is not merely referring to the arbitrariness of taking a particular point rather than a neighboring one, for example, twenty-one rather than eighteen or twenty-three years: "I am talking about the absence of any compelling rationale to draw the line in the neighborhood of twenty-one rather than eleven or thirty-one."[11]

Schrag's remarks raise two questions. First, does the argument from "actual" moral agency provide a compelling basis for drawing the age line where it is currently drawn (eighteen years)? Second, if not, where should the line be drawn, that is, does the argument compel us to draw the line at some point or other in the sequence from infancy to old age?

In answer to my first question, the argument tells us that the rationale for drawing the line where it is presently drawn is that this secures the freedom of all and only those who are moral agents—the assumption being that *only* those who are eighteen years of age and over are moral agents. I agree with Schrag that this assumption is preposterous. Surely, there is ample evidence to prove that even very young children possess the capacity to formulate plans and to execute them independently. I suspect, however, that most of the burden for the claim that children are not moral agents is put on the shoulders of the implied notion of the capacity to self-legislate rules. But even here there is evidence that most children above the age of thirteen or fourteen years have this capacity. I have in mind Lawrence Kohlberg's studies of moral development in children.[12] In order to make these studies relevant to the question of whether children in certain age ranges have the capacity to be self-legislating, let us suppose that what is meant by the notion of "understanding and adopting moral rules" is at least to possess the ability to base one's evaluation of the rightness and wrongness of moral dilemma situations on such rules as "Do not steal," "Do not lie," etc., and to be prone to feel guilty when one breaks one of these rules oneself. Now this in fact describes the fourth stage of moral development distinguished by Kohlberg. Although he believes that one cannot associate any one stage of moral development with adolescence, his studies of middle-class urban boys in the United States indicate that many have attained this stage at age thirteen and that it represents the second highest stage arrived at by those at age sixteen, with the highest percentage in the latter group having attained the fifth or "principled" stage of moral development in which "the individual . . . is much more willing to view the law as flexible and changing, as long as these changes follow rational deliberations and considerations of social utility and are based on consensus."[13]

It follows that if we are to accept the relevance of Kohlberg's data to the question whether some age groups of children are self-legislating beings, then most children above the age of thirteen years are self-legislating. Since they are also self-determining beings, it follows that most members of this group of children are moral agents. To return to Professor Schrag's remarks, I disagree with his claim that there is no rationale that compels us to draw the age line somewhere in the sequence from infancy to old age. My point is that the argument from "actual" moral agency contains such a rationale. Moreover, as noted above, there is some empirical evidence that is relevant to the question of where the age line is to be drawn. However, I agree with Schrag that the evidence does not show that the age line is to be drawn at the current "age of majority" (eighteen years). In short, premise (1b) of the argument from "actual" moral agency is false.

Moral Agency and Natural Rights. The claim advanced in premise (1a) is that a necessary condition for possessing natural N-rights is that one has the status of moral agent, that is, one is a being with an autonomous will. Notice, however, that no reason whatsoever is given for the alleged necessary connection between natural N-rights and autonomy of will. It is especially urgent to argue this point if one considers that our ordinary moral intuitions about children incline us to suppose that they possess at least *some* moral negative rights, and this is so regardless of how we settle the issue of whether they have an autonomous will. Thus, most of us would insist that if there are any moral (natural) rights at all, *all* human beings (children included) have the moral right not to be tortured or treated cruelly, and we would take it as irrelevant that some members of the class of human beings—young children, for instance—do not have an autonomous will. In short, there is no *relevant* respect in which children differ from adults such that members of the latter class can be said to have this moral right whereas others lack it.

There are ways in which proponents of the "actual" moral agency argument might try to avoid this difficulty. First, one might "stick to one's guns" and argue that our ordinary moral intuitions about the moral or natural rights of young children are wrong. One might argue in this way because he finds persuasive arguments that establish a necessary connection between moral rights and autonomy of will. Consider the following argument. Suppose it is held that an autonomous will is the highest good, so that an autonomous will is an end in itself and should be treated as such. Now we can treat a faculty of some being as an end in itself only by treating the being himself as an end. And because only a being who can formulate and adopt moral rules, that is, a moral agent, can possess an autonomous will, it follows that only moral agents have the right to be treated as ends.[14]

This argument is invalid. Young children do not have the desirable faculty of an autonomous will, but they have the right to be treated as an end. For example, we would think it a violation of a young child's moral rights if she were subjected to cruel treatment by her parents. Thus, even if we admit that an autonomous will is the highest good, all that this entails is that it is desirable to possess this faculty. It does not follow that *only* those beings who have this (desirable) faculty have the right to be treated as ends.

A second way to respond to the objection to premise (1a) is to make a revision in the original argument, replacing premise (1a) with the following premise:

(2a) If a being has the natural N-right "not to be harmed in his liberty," then he or she is a moral agent.

That is, instead of asserting that moral agency is a necessary condition of possessing *any* sort of natural, negative right, the argument is revised so that it makes the more modest claim that one must be a moral agent to possess the *particular* negative right to the forbearance of those who would constrain him in doing what he wants or chooses to do.

Is premise (2a) true? It is difficult to discover a plausible argument in support of it. Thus, it might be argued that moral agency is a necessary condition for the possession of this right because only moral agents are capable of enjoying freedom of action. But, as Herbert Spencer pointed out long ago,[15] this is false. Young children are as capable of enjoying liberty as adults, although the actions they enjoy are often different from the kinds of activities enjoyed by adults.

This leads me to suspect that what is in fact being proposed by defenders of the argument from "actual" moral agency is a premise even more particular in content than (2a). It is that there is a peculiar *kind* of liberty that moral agents enjoy and it is this kind that has moral agency as its necessary condition. The favored candidate is "the special, *moral* freedom of man to guide his actions by his sense of right and wrong."[16] That is, what is in fact being advanced is the following premise:

(2b) If a being has the natural N-right not to be constrained in the exercise of his moral freedom, then he or she is a moral agent.

The idea in premise (2b) is that when we talk about a moral agent's right to liberty, what we really have in mind to protect is the freedom to be self-determining and self-legislating.

Premise (2b) is more plausible than (2a), but it wins this advantage only because beings who are *not* moral agents *by definition* lack the capacity for self-determination and self-legislation. Hence, it would make no sense to ascribe to them the moral right to the corresponding activities. In general, if a being is the *kind* of being who lacks the capacity to engage in a particular activity, then there would not be any sense to ascribing to this person the right to engage in that activity. In my concluding remarks to this chapter, I shall say more about whether the observation in premise (2b) about the logical connection between natural N-rights and natural capacities leads us to draw any important conclusions about the legal A-liberties that ought to be possessed by children.

The Argument from "Potential" Moral Agency

Instead of opposing our intuitions about the moral rights of children, many philosophers will attempt to account for them by slightly altering the preceding theory about the conditions necessary for possessing natural N-rights. Thus, it has been argued that although children are not moral agents, they uniquely possess the *potential* for developing into beings with autonomous will.[17] Moreover, the fact that children are potential moral agents is sufficient for ascribing to them at least some moral claim rights. In general, it is sufficient to establish their right to be provided the conditions that will allow them to *become* beings who are self-determining and self-legislating.

The latter right entails not only the negative rights not to be harmed, abused, or treated cruelly, but also the positive rights to be cared for and protected by others. That is, if a child's potential to become an autonomous being is to be realized, then it is necessary not only to refrain from acts that will prevent him from realizing this potential, but we must *do* certain positive acts to help him attain his potential even if this means forcing him to follow certain self-developing pursuits. In short, his potential to develop into a moral agent justifies many kinds of paternalistic interferences that we would never think justified in the case of adults. "We make an exception of children because we think they have not got the knowledge and experience to make any choice worthy of the name, and also because there are some talents which have to be cultivated young if at all, so that the adult's ability to make a valid choice (one with plenty of possibilities) itself depends on early restrictions of liberty."[18]*

Indeed, it would be a violation of a child's moral rights if we did *not* compel him to do or refrain from doing certain things, for example, to be educated or to refrain from drinking alcoholic beverages. Adults have a *duty* to force or compel children to do those acts that will aid them in becoming autonomous beings and to refrain from doing those acts that will hinder them in attaining their goal, and this (natural) duty is derived from the child's (natural) right to be provided the conditions that will allow him to realize his potential to become an autonomous being.

I argued in the preceding section that Kantian considerations about "actual" moral agents could not be used to support the proposition that the

*Herbert Morris expresses similar views about the moral importance of developing a child's potential to become a person in the following passage:

> Children possess the right to be treated as persons but they possess this right as an individual might be said in the law of property to possess a future interest. There are advantages in talking of individuals as having a right though complete enjoyment of it is postponed. Brought to our attention, if we ascribe to them the right, is the legitimacy of their complaint if they are not provided with opportunities and conditions assuring their full enjoyment of the right when they acquire the characteristics of persons. More than this, all persons are charged with the sensitive task of not denying them the right to be a person and to be treated as a person by failing to provide the conditions for their becoming individuals who are able freely and in an informed way to choose and who are prepared themselves to assume responsibility for their choices. There is an obligation imposed upon us all, unlike that we have with respect to animals, to respond to children in such a way as to maximize the chances of their becoming persons. This may well impose upon us the obligation to treat them as persons from a very early age, that is, to respect their choices and to place upon them the responsibility for the choices to be made. There is no need to say that there is a close connection between how we respond to them and what they become. It also imposes upon us all the duty to display constantly the qualities of a person, for what they become they will largely become because of what they learn from us is acceptable behavior. ["Persons and Punishment," in *Human Rights,* A. I. Melden (Belmont, Calif.; Wadsworth, 1970), pp. 127-28]

state is justified in granting legal C-claims to children, for the sphere of legally enforceable rights is confined to natural N-rights. However, there is no such bar to granting legal C-claims to children to be found in the preceding considerations about "potential" moral agents. Indeed, these considerations not only give support to the proposition that the state is justified in granting legal C-claims, but they support the stronger claim that the state has a duty to do this, for the state would be violating the right of children to have their potential to become moral agents developed if it were to deny them legal C-claims.

Second, we get a considerably different and more detailed argument for the proposition that the state is justified in denying legal A-liberties to children from that provided by the argument from "actual" moral agency. The argument has the following structure:

(3a) Children are potential moral agents.

(3b) If a being is a potential moral agent, then he has the natural right to be provided the conditions that will allow him to develop into a moral agent.

(3c) If a being has the natural right to be provided the conditions that will allow him to develop into a moral agent, then he has the right to be treated paternalistically by others, that is, to be compelled to do or refrain from doing those acts that might enhance or reduce his chances of developing into a moral agent.

Therefore,

(3d) A child has the right to be treated paternalistically.

If we grant that the state would fulfill its duty to treat children paternalistically by denying legal A-liberties to children, then it follows that

(3e) It is justifiable for the state to deny legal A-liberties to children.

Moral Rights and Potential Persons

Is the preceding argument sound? The weakest point in the argument is premise (3b). The claim in (3b) is that potential moral agency is a sufficient condition of a particular kind of moral right. Although this is unlike the claim in premise (1a) that moral agency is a necessary condition of natural N-rights, the same criticism applies. If it is not clear what it is about moral agency that provides a necessary connection for possessing moral rights, then neither is it clear what it is about *potential* moral agency that provides a sufficient condition for possession of the moral claim right to be provided the conditions needed to develop this potential. Mere possession of the potential to become an X is not taken as sufficient to establish that one has the right to be provided the conditions that will help one to become an X. Counterexamples are not hard to find. Suppose that P has the potential to become a terrorist or an assassin. We would not maintain that P has the claim right to have this potential brought to actuality. Indeed, we would probably assert that others would have the duty to see to it that P not actualize his potential.

Defenders of premise (3b) may reply to this objection by arguing that their move from potentiality to possession of moral rights only holds for the specific potentiality *to become a moral agent*. It does not hold for other sorts of things that beings may have the potential to become. But this is again too strong a condition, for it would make it a violation of the rights of *any* being who has the potential to become a moral agent to deprive him of the conditions for becoming a moral agent. Thus, it would not only be a violation of this moral right to abort a fetus at any stage after conception, but it would be a violation of this moral right to practice contraception at all. For in either case it could be argued that one had prevented what had the *potential* to become a moral agent from actually developing into one. Now this consideration will not pose a difficulty for those who believe that child abuse, abortion, and contraception are all morally wrong (none morally worse than the others), but most persons are inclined to think that at least some abortions and all cases of contraception are not a violation of moral claim rights.[19]

Conclusion

Both the argument from "actual" moral agency and the argument from "potential" moral agency are seriously flawed. The argument from "actual" moral agency is unsound because it contains the false premise that children are not moral agents. Moreover, even if we revise this premise to apply to only those young children of whom we can say with some assurance that they lack an autonomous will, the argument still fails because of premise (1b). It is false to assert that moral agency is a necessary condition for the possession of moral negative rights. Children have some moral negative rights (such as not to be harmed or abused) the possession of which has nothing to do with possession or lack of autonomy of will.

The argument from potential moral agency does somewhat better, although premise (3b) of that argument commits the same error as premise (1b) of the argument from moral agency, for it implies that some children are not moral agents. And again, if I revise the argument so that it applies only to very young children, the argument gets into difficulty by virtue of the false claim that the potential to be a moral agent is a sufficient condition of the moral right to be provided the conditions for developing this potential.

Is there anything to be salvaged from either of these arguments? First, I have conceded that *some* children are not moral agents. Although I do not think that possession of the complex characteristic of moral agency is relevant to the question whether a being has many of the moral claim rights we normally ascribe to persons, possession of the capacity to be self-determining is relevant to the question whether a being *has* certain *moral* liberty and power rights and to the question whether a being *ought to be granted legal* A-liberties.

In general, to say of a being that he has the right to moral freedom implies that he has the (rational) capacity to make moral choices. Hence, it would make no sense to say of a two-year-old child that he has the right to decide (say) whether he ought to be given a blood transfusion during surgery: he lacks the capacity to adopt and act on moral reasons applicable to a case of this type.

Similar (though somewhat different) considerations apply to the question of whether legal A-liberties and legal powers ought to be granted to very young children. If it is clear that the age group in question lacks the capacity to make a certain kind of choice, then although we could (logically) grant them the relevant liberties and powers, it is clear that there would be no point in doing this. That is, we might give young children the legal right to vote, to make contracts and wills, and to marry, but one reason for refusing to do this is not that it would be logically impossible to do it, but simply because they (infants) are incapable of ever exercising such rights.

At the beginning of this chapter I raised the question of whether there is a sound argument for the proposition that the state is justified in denying legal A-liberties to children. Critical examination of the arguments from "actual" and "potential" moral agency only yields the relatively minor point that one must have the intellectual capacity to exercise a legal A-liberty in order for there to be a point in granting it to him. But (*a*) this applies only to very young children, and (*b*) it has nothing to do with whether or not such children are moral agents in the full sense of this term (that is, beings with an autonomous will). Hence, for children who have the capacity to exercise legal A-liberties we are still without an adequate answer to the question of whether it is justifiable for the state to deny such rights to them. I now turn to a set of more plausible replies to this question.

5 *Beneficence and Rational Choice*

The natural alternative to the arguments from moral agency is a teleological argument for denying certain legal liberty and power rights to children and for granting them certain positive claims. There are several kinds of teleological argument that we might construct, but what they have in common is the thesis that moral rights function, not to mark out a characteristic of some human beings (such as possession of an autonomous will), but rather to mark out which of all moral claims ought to be enforced by the state. On this view, a being may be said to have a right to X if and only if the state ought to defend him in the possession of X, all things considered.[1] Hence, unlike the argument from moral agency, teleological arguments are alike in agreeing that moral rights are *not* morally basic. They are *derivative* from more general moral principles.

Suppose, for example, that we adopt the principle of beneficence. To state it roughly, this is the principle that we have a duty to prevent harm or evil and to promote good.[2*] We then use this principle to arrive at a set of rights that the state ought to guarantee to persons as a matter of law. For example, everyone has the right not to be assaulted because the state has the duty to prevent harm or evil and it would be a violation of this duty if it did not guarantee this right to persons as a matter of law.

The same considerations can be used to answer the question of whether children ought to be granted those liberty and power rights that the state normally grants to its adult members (that is, legal A-liberties). Suppose,

*The accurate statement of the principle is made by William Frankena, *Ethics*, 2nd ed. (Englewood Cliffs, N.J.: Prentice-Hall, 1973), p. 47:
What does the principle of beneficence say? Four things, I think:
1. One ought not to inflict evil or harm (what is bad).
2. One ought to prevent evil or harm.
3. One ought to remove evil.
4. One ought to do or promote good.

for example, that we are asked to justify, on teleological grounds, the common practice of denying to children the legal right to purchase alcoholic beverages. First, we accept the common belief that children lack the capacity for rational choice. Second, we contend that this fact is relevant *only* because it shows that there are very real and personal harms that may befall a child if he or she is allowed the freedom to purchase and consume alcohol. Unlike the arguments from moral agency, the focus is no longer on the question of whether children have moral or natural rights, but simply on whether according them a legal right will promote good or prevent evil. Paternalistic interferences in the lives of children are justifiable only because the state has a duty of beneficence and this duty is fulfilled by adopting and enacting paternalistic laws.

The principle of beneficence can also be used to justify the practice of granting legal C-claims to children. Since children lack the rational capacity needed to provide for and protect themselves, they would suffer harm or fail to promote their own good unless the state required parents (by enforcing legal C-claims) to provide for and protect them. This being so, and since the state has a duty of beneficence, it follows that the state has a duty to grant legal C-claims to children.

Clarification of the Argument

I shall call the preceding argument for denying legal A-liberties and granting legal C-claims to children the "argument from beneficence." However, in this chapter I discuss only that part of the argument that would deny legal A-liberties to children. Let me begin by considering its schematic detail:

(1a) There is a duty of beneficence, and this duty is violated by failing either to promote good or to prevent harm or evil.

(1b) If children are granted legal A-liberties, then (as a result) many of them will suffer harm or will fail to advance their own good or welfare.

Therefore,

(1c) The state would violate the duty of beneficence if it should grant legal A-liberties to children.

Therefore,

(1d) It is justifiable for the state to deny legal A-liberties to children.

Of course, the conclusion (1d) could be restated to assert the stronger claim that the state *ought* to deny legal A-liberties to children. But since the weaker conclusion is all that is required of an argument for denying legal rights to children, I shall stay with it.

There are several points of clarification to make about the argument. First, the statements in premises (1a) and (1b) mention two alternatives: preventing harm or promoting good (or welfare). It would have been possible to state the case more simply by referring only to the promotion of good, but it is useful to distinguish cases in which we interfere with liberty where the good referred to is not being harmed from cases in which the good referred to is some positive benefit we hope to achieve. That is, not being harmed is assuredly a benefit, but there are some benefits we can achieve over and above not being harmed. For example, compulsory school attendance laws are justified partly on the ground that it is to the child's positive benefit that he be made to go to school, and this is not just another way of saying that he will be harmed if he does not attend (though this may be an indirect result of his not receiving the benefit).

The second point to make about the argument is that premise (1b) is a prediction about what will happen to children under certain conditions. As such, it can be verified by gathering relevant statistical data. This is rarely, if ever, done. Usually, a claim of the sort made in statement (1b) is derived from a more general empirical claim about the likelihood of harm's being caused to beings who "lack the capacity for rational choice" or, to employ a concept used in the last chapter, to beings who are not "self-determining." That is, the following subargument stands behind premise (1b):

(2a) If beings who lack the capacity for rational choice are granted legal A-liberties, then (as a result) many of them will suffer harm or will fail to advance their own good.

(2b) Children are beings who lack the capacity for rational choice.

Therefore,

(1b) If children are granted legal A-liberties, then (as a result) many of them will suffer harm or will fail to advance their own good or welfare.

Notice that premise (2b) employs the notion of "capacity for rational choice" rather than "capacity for self-determination." This is because the former notion makes statement (2b) more *plausible* and it is a capacity the presence or absence of which is more *relevant* to the question of whether the principle of beneficence dictates paternalistic intervention in the lives of children. I argued in the last chapter that only very young children can plausibly be said to lack the capacity for self-determination, for only they are unable to formulate or execute plans on their own. But even though most children are self-determining, the proponent of the argument from beneficence would still want to insist that children are more likely than competent adults to perform self-harm-causing actions. And he thinks this because he thinks that they lack the further capacity to formulate *rational* plans or to execute these plans in a *rational* manner. That is, it is not that children cannot formulate and execute plans or purposes that should trouble us (he would argue) but that they lack or fail to possess to an adequate degree the capacity for *rational* choice.

The final thing to note about the argument from beneficence is that it does not employ the notion of "consent" of the being or beings whose freedom of action is being legally restricted. The justification of intervention is stated entirely in terms of the child's own good, regardless of whether or not he or she wants or desires to have this good promoted. Nor does the argument imply anything about the "hypothetical" consent of the person whose freedom is restricted. It may be that the child interfered with would want us to do what we are now doing if he or she were a competent adult, but the argument from beneficence is silent about such claims and we need not infer them from it.

The Principle of Beneficence

There is a great deal that is objectionable in the argument from beneficence for denying legal A-liberties to children. The obvious objection is that not only can a case be made for the claim in premise (1c), but that an equally good case can be made for the claim that the state violates the duty of beneficence when it fails to deny certain liberty rights to competent adults. For example, mountain climbing is said to be an activity that is likely to bring about death or serious injury to the unchaperoned amateur climber. If this is so, then the principle of beneficence requires us to deny such adults the liberty right to climb mountains. And yet although we might agree that the state should continually confront potential climbers with the facts about the risks involved in climbing mountains, most of us would resist the suggestion that the unchaperoned amateur should be legally prevented from climbing mountains on the *sole* ground that this is likely to lead to his death or serious injury.

There are two ways to avoid this objection. First, it might be argued that the principle of beneficence places a priority on the duty to promote good so that where this duty comes into conflict with the duty to prevent harm the former takes precedence. Thus, by not denying competent adults the right to climb mountains, for instance, we promote good in that they are made to practice making difficult choices (for instance, whether or not to climb mountains), and this in turn aids them in bringing to full development some of their mental powers. Hence, although harm may result from making a choice to climb mountains, since the duty to promote good takes precedence over the duty to prevent harm, the competent adult must be allowed the right to climb mountains.

One might wonder whether the same considerations might be used to press for children to be granted the right to climb mountains, or indeed to be granted at least some of the rights found in the class of legal A-liberties. Isn't it the case that some children (for example, older children) would benefit (in the way that adults benefit) by being allowed to make some of those choices now legally denied to them? I shall return to this question in the next chapter. For now I want to cast doubt on the prior assumption that, other things being equal, the duty to promote good takes precedence over the duty to prevent harm. There are many examples to the contrary. Suppose that I can save you from drowning by rowing a boat out to the middle of the lake, but that by taking the time to do this I miss the opportunity to do something that would benefit another. We would hardly argue that the duty to do the latter (supposing that it is a duty) takes precedence over the duty to do the former, other things being equal.

The second way to avoid the original objection to the principle of beneficence is more plausible, but it amounts to an abandonment of the principle. Thus, it might be suggested that, since the duty to prevent harm comes into conflict with the duty to promote good whenever we are deciding whether to grant or deny a particular legal liberty right to a class of individuals, we should attempt to bring about the greatest *balance* of good over evil. Thus, we might argue that the quantity of good likely to be produced is greater than the quantity of evil likely to be produced by refraining from enacting legislation that would deny competent adults the right to climb mountains, whereas the balance of good over evil is in the other direction when we consider the case of children and legal A-liberties.

Although this is a more plausible solution to the original objection, it must be pointed out that it effectively replaces the principle of beneficence with the principle of *utility*. The latter principle is stated in quantitative terms and presupposes that goods and evils can be measured and balanced in some way. The principle of beneficence does not deny this, but neither does it imply this.

I conclude, then, that the original objection to the principle of beneficence stands. It is too broad to be an adequate principle upon which to make decisions about what sorts of legal liberty/power right to grant to classes of individuals, and so it cannot be used to guide our decision making about the legal liberty and liberty/power rights of children.

The Capacity for Rational Choice

Although I have said enough to expose a fatal flaw in the argument from beneficence, I confess to an urge to continue and use the argument as a vehicle for discussion of an assumption common to all of the remaining arguments to be discussed in succeeding chapters. This is the assumption that the relevant difference between children and adults justifying the different treatment received by each under the law is that the former lack "the capacity for rational choice." In the argument from beneficence this assumption occurs as premise (2b) of the subargument designed to establish the prediction that children will suffer harm or will fail to promote their own good if granted legal A-liberties. It will be seen to play an equally crucial role in the argument from utility (chapter 6) and the argument from the social contract (chapter 7).

There are two questions that I wish to ask about this assumption. First, what does it *mean* to say that a person or class of persons has or lacks "the capacity for rational choice"? Second, what *evidence*, if any, do we have to prove that in fact children lack the capacity for rational choice?

There is a distinction between the notion of a *correct* choice and that of a *reasonable* choice.[3] In the former case we mean that the choice could somehow be supported on rational grounds, that is, it could be shown that there were good reasons for making it, even if those reasons had never entered the head of the person who made it. Thus, a happy-go-lucky gambler may impulsively bet a few dollars on a horse and win. Although he could not, at the time, support his choice on rational grounds, he made the *correct* choice: evidence potentially available (such causally relevant factors as form and weather conditions, perhaps) would show this.

However, when we say that a choice is *reasonable* we mean to refer to the choice made by the person on the basis of evidence presently available to him. For example, a mature, informed business executive may ponder for days about a potential investment and yet make a financially disastrous choice. Although his choice was not correct (it could be shown that there were good reasons for not making it), given the evidence available to him, that choice was the reasonable one to make. Moreover, in saying that it was "the reasonable one to make," we suggest that it was the choice that a reasonable person would have made, had his knowledge about the relevant circumstances been the same as that of the chooser's.

What do we mean when we call the choices of children "irrational"? Some examples: my seven-year-old son chooses to wear a light shirt out-of-doors on a cold and windy day; he chooses to ride his bicycle on a busy street; he wants to stay home from school today; he would prefer to eat nothing but ice cream for supper this evening. In calling each of these choices (decisions, wants, preferences) irrational, I *may* be saying that his choice is not correct (that it cannot be supported on rational grounds), but I am more likely to mean that any reasonable person, similarly situated, would *not* make that sort of choice. What seems troublesome about the choices that some children (and some adults) make is that although they frequently have the same evidence available to them that we have, they attach incorrect evaluative weights to the relevant facts. For example, my child *knows* that it is below 5° C. today, that his shirt is light weight, and that he might catch cold as a result (I *told* him this), but he magnifies or distorts the discomfort of wearing a sweater, and catching a cold is too remote a possibility for him to consider seriously.

This is not to discount the problems inherent in adopting a "reasonable person" standard of rational choice. Thus, we must be careful not to make the child's cognitive and emotional capacities part of the "circumstances" in which the reasonable person is to be situated, for then the question What would a reasonable person have chosen in the same circumstances? will always receive the answer He would have chosen exactly what the child chose. What is wanted is an "objective" standard of reasonableness; that is, the reasonable person must be given some attributes that do not correspond to those of the individual child in showing that the latter has failed to make a reasonable choice. We endow the reasonable person with the "normal" cognitive and emotional capacities of the competent adult instead of the special capacities of the (average) child.

Third, in order to decide whether there is a satisfactory empirical basis for the claim that children lack the capacity to make rational choices, we must decide what sort of choices *would* be made by reasonable persons in a variety of circumstances, and this, of course, is an enormously complex task; it depends on the construction of a general view about ideal development, the goals it is desirable for people to attain—in short, an "ethical opinion about the 'true' nature of Man."[4] Thus, if it is good for persons to attain certain moral or nonmoral virtues or excellences, then a reasonable choice (a choice of a reasonable person) will be one that reflects or promotes these virtues. Of course, the difficulty with such "general views" is that they force a person to determine that certain values are themselves reasonable. Since value theorists are so divided as to whether or not there is a method of settling this question, let alone what it is, I shall not attempt to argue for a general theory of value here. Nonetheless, there are surely *some* things that will command our assent as things that it is reasonable to pursue. Thus, most people would agree that survival is a proper end of human activity. If this is so, we may refer to most choices that put a person in danger of losing his life or risking serious harm or injury as unreasonable or irrational choices—choices that reasonable persons would not make. Since this is the sort of choice that most people have in mind when they refer to a child's lack of capacity to make rational choices, we now have one question that might be settled empirically: "Do children lack the capacity to make the sort of choice that would not put them in danger of risking loss of life or serious bodily harm?"

However, before attempting to answer this question, we must decide what is meant by the phrase "lacks the capacity." If a particular choice is of the sort that a reasonable person with normal capacities *would* have made in similar circumstances, then how are we to understand the further assertion "Children *lack the capacity* to make that sort of choice"?

I suspect that what is *sometimes* meant (intended) by this assertion is simply that children are *not prone* to make reasonable choices, that is, if placed in certain sorts of situations and faced with certain alternatives, they do not make choices that are reasonable (using the preceding standard of reasonableness). However, when we speak of the lack of capacity for rational choice, if the phrase "lack of capacity" is being used correctly, we mean to assert more than this, namely, that children *cannot* make rational choices. Of course, to say that so-and-so cannot make rational choices implies that he is not prone to make rational choices, but the latter statement does not imply the former. If he is not prone to make rational choices, then it is not a good bet that he will make them (we don't expect him to make them). But if he cannot make rational choices, then it is a certainty that he won't make them. Moreover, the evidence for asserting the former is often different from what we would offer in support of the latter. Thus, it would be enough to prove that someone is not prone to make rational choices to show that he is not willing to do this. But to say that he is not willing to make rational choices is consistent with saying that he *can* make rational choices (if he wants)!

Do Children Lack the Capacity for Rational Choice?

The upshot of the preceding remarks is that the question Do children lack the capacity for rational choice? is best divided into two questions: (*a*) what choice *would* a reasonable person with normal capacities make in circumstances of type X? and (*b*) *can* children with *their* capacities make that choice? Moreover, I suggested that in order to give a focus to question *(a),* we should assume that if X is a situation in which a possible choice could lead to death or serious injury, then that sort of choice is unreasonable; in other words, it is not the choice that a reasonable person with normal capacities would make. Hence, the empirical question that we should now attempt to answer is a variation of question (*b*): *can* children with *their* capacities make choices that do not put at risk their life or bodily integrity?

I said that one interpretation of this question is: are children prone to put themselves in situations in which their survival or bodily integrity is put at risk? In order to answer this question in the affirmative, we must be prepared to cite relevant statistical data. However, existing empirical research does not seem to prove very much.

First, experimental work in child psychology is usually done in a laboratory setting that does not reflect the real social situations in which the child may find himself.* Second, existing statistical studies on causes of death in the U.S. population, although more relevant to our question, are inconclusive. They show that whereas accidents are the leading cause of death among children over the age of one year, accidents rank fourth in causes of death among the total population.[5] Are we to conclude from this that children are more prone to put themselves in situations in which their survival or bodily integrity is at risk? Or shall we conclude that children are not as susceptible as the rest of the population to heart disease, cancer, and stroke (the three leading causes of death)? This is not to deny that some young children, when left unattended, will ride tricycles in the street, play with matches, and drink strange substances that turn out to be poison. But we can no more conclude from this that *all* persons legally classified as children are prone to do such things than we can draw the conclusion that all adults are prone to endanger themselves from the fact that some adults chain-smoke cigarettes, sky dive, or climb mountains.

I have argued that the assertion that children lack the capacity for rational choice is not normally taken to be the claim that they are not prone to do this. Rather, it is more often put forward as the stronger assertion that they are *not able* to make reasonable choices. What evidence do we have for this? The general empirical judgments that are usually appealed to in advancing this claim are these: (3a) those who lack the *information* that

*Arlene Skolnik argues that American developmental psychology "has tended to emphasize laboratory studies in which the child performs an unfamiliar task in a strange situation with a strange adult." The bits of information that we get from such studies are so isolated that they do not reflect the real situations from which they were supposedly derived ("The Limits of Childhood," *Law and Contemporary Problems* 39 [1975]: 53).

there is a risk of harm involved in some of the alternative courses of action open to them cannot make reasonable choices; (4a) those who lack the *cognitive capacity to understand* that there is a risk of harm involved in a particular choice cannot make reasonable choices; and (5a) those who are unable to *defer the gratification of a desire* for very long cannot make reasonable choices. We then couple each of these general judgments with the following particular judgments: (3b) children lack information about the risks of harm involved in many of their choices; (4b) children lack the cognitive capacity to understand that there is a risk of harm involved in many of their choices; and (5b) children are unable to defer gratifying their desires for very long. From each pair of judgments (3a and 3b, 4a and 4b, 5a and 5b) we derive the conclusion that children cannot make reasonable choices. That is, premise (2b) of the subargument from beneficence has been proved true.

The general empirical judgments in statements (3a), (4a), and (5a) appear to be true. If I am asked to give a reason for my claim that I cannot make a reasonable choice in a given situation, then it would suffice to say either that I do not have the relevant information or that I cannot understand certain pieces of information or that I cannot defer the gratification of a desire. In short, each of these states a plausible sufficient condition for being unable to make a reasonable choice between alternative courses of action.

However, I would strongly object to the claims made in statements (3b), (4b), and (5b). Either there is no evidence available to support the claim made in each case or the evidence that is available will support the claim only if it is qualified to apply to very young children. For example, if the ability to discriminate shape is present in a child from as early as six months of age,* and if children have been shown to reach the highest stage of human

*This assertion is made by B. C. Ling ("Form Discrimination As a Learning Cue in Infants," *Comparative Psychology Monograph* 17, no. 86 [Baltimore: Williams and Wilkens, 1941], pp. 519–620). Ling's subjects were fifty children, six to fifteen months of age. They identified and isolated a property of an object—its triangularity, for example—that served to differentiate it in form from some other object. They then ascribed that property to other forms (triangles), where appropriate, even when those forms were larger or smaller than the first, or upside down.

What concepts of size, space, time, number, life, self, and other persons children possess at various age levels has been rather thoroughly established. Such information has been utilized to determine age norms for various concepts in intelligence tests (L. M. Terman and M. E. Merrill, *Measuring Intelligence* [New York: Houghton Mifflin, 1937]). At the nine-year-old level, for example, children are normally able to tell how the objects in each of the following pairs are alike and how they are different: honey and glue, pencil and pen, banana and lemon, shoe and glove. By the age of eleven years, they are expected to define such abstract words as "connection" and "obedience" (W. E. Martin and C. B. Stendler, *Child Behavior and Development* [New York: Harcourt, Brace and World, 1959], p. 524).

cognitive development "at about age twelve,"[6]* then it is difficult to believe the claim in statement (4b) that all children (that is, all persons up to the age of eighteen years) lack the cognitive capacity to understand that there is a risk of harm involved in a choice that is available to them. Second, the psychological studies of the behavior of children in games indicate a capacity at a very young age to defer immediate gratification of a desire. Indeed, children in the five-to-seven-year age range "come to see the necessity for rules and sometimes set up much stricter regulations governing their own activities than those established by adults."[7] The strong urge to gratify a desire to take a ball and run is resisted by the child who knows that the rules of the game do not allow this.† Third, the proposal in statement (3b) that children lack the information about the risks involved in many of their choices is undoubtedly true about a larger age range of children than the range for which the claims in statements (4b) and (5b) are true. However, since there are no studies available to indicate precisely what sorts of informational lack exists at specific age ranges, there is not much more to be done than to make educated guesses about the age ranges. At what age, for example, do children acquire the information that there are risks involved in being in certain areas of large American cities at night? At what age do they learn that there are hazards involved in operating certain kinds of machinery? The answers to these questions often depend upon the extent to which adults have chosen to withhold such information from them. Nonetheless, it is difficult to believe that most city children beyond the age of say, ten years, are ignorant of the former fact and that most farm children of the same age are ignorant of the latter fact.

I conclude that because the claims made in statements (3b), (4b), and (5b) are unfounded, the arguments in which these claims occur as premises are unsound and so do not serve as grounds for the claim in statement (2b) that most children lack the capacity for rational choice. However, this is not to deny that some children lack this capacity. The preceding considerations

*Piaget describes this as the stage of "formal operations" in which the child is able to use "binary operations" (e.g., "negation," "conjunction," or "conjunctive negation") and solve scientific problems such as identifying factors affecting a pendulum's frequency of oscillation. Children normally reach an earlier stage, described by Piaget as the stage of "concrete operations," between ages seven and eleven. At this stage he finds that they are able to do such things as combine subclasses into supraclasses (e.g., "A is larger than B and B is larger than C" is combined into a new statement "A is larger than C") and reverse mathematical operations (B. Inhelder and J. Piaget, *The Growth of Logical Thinking*, trans. A. Parsons and S. Milgram [New York: Basic Books, 1958]).

†However, children have a tendency to yield to group pressure against their own better judgment that does not decline to adult levels until around age sixteen (Joy M. N. Query, "The Influence of Group Pressures on the Judgments of Children and Adolescents: A Comparative Study," *Adolescence* 3 [1968]: 153–60).

not only support the claim that there is no evidence to show that most children do not possess the capacity for rational choice, but they give some support for the claim that *some* children do not possess this capacity. What the empirical data do not tell us is the precise age range within which we can contend that some children lack the capacity to make rational choices.

Finally, it may be objected to the above that the crucial point is a *developmental* one. That is, since a person can possess more or less of the capacity to make a rational choice, then the question I should have been asking all along is not whether children have the capacity for rational choice but whether children have this capacity to an adequate degree. But surely the standard of adequacy must be specified before the latter question can be answered, and in the context of the preceding discussion, I submit that to say that X has the capacity for rational choice to an "adequate degree" means that X is able to make choices that are not self-harm risking. It should be obvious that the question of whether children have the latter ability *is* the question I have been asking all along, that is, I find no real distinction between the two questions put in the second sentence of this paragraph.

Conclusion

The main reason that the argument from beneficence fails to give adequate support to the claim that the state is justified in denying legal A-liberties to children is that the principle of beneficence is too broad to be of much use in deciding whether or not to grant legal rights to any class of persons, including children. Since laws conferring legal rights will rarely bring about only good and not produce any evil, it would seem that we would always violate the principle of beneficence by enacting such laws.

The second reason the argument from beneficence fails is that it assumes, without adequate empirical support, that children lack the capacity for rational choice. I take this to mean that children cannot make choices that are reasonable (where the standard of reasonable choice is the likelihood of self-harm). But the evidence that is available will only support this claim if applied to very young children. In any case it does not give any support to the claim that children over the age of thirteen or fourteen years lack the capacity for rational choice.

What this shows, I believe, is the critical need for empirical research in this area. If we seriously wish to advance an argument for denying legal A-liberties to children and we base it in part on the claim that children lack certain relevant capacities, then we must be prepared to support that claim with hard, empirical evidence. This is never done. Instead, what is usually presented are "educated guesses" about what children would do or would fail to do if left to their own devices. But we would not allow such guesses to be used as the sole support of claims made in an argument designed to justify paternalistic restrictions on *adult* liberties. (The demand for data in the ongoing debate on the legalization of marijuana is a case in point.) We owe children at least as much consideration when deciding what liberty rights to grant or deny to them.

6 The Argument from Utility

I have argued that we will not be able to meet the ideal of the principle of beneficence in the process of adopting laws that confer legal rights, for such laws will rarely bring about only good and not produce any evil. Hence, we are forced to compromise with this ideal by adopting only those rights-conferring laws that bring about the best possible balance of good over evil.

Let us replace the principle of beneficence with a principle that tells us that our duty is to bring about the greatest possible balance of good over evil in the universe. Let us suppose further that "good" means happiness (or pleasure) and "evil" means misery (or pain). The result is the hedonist version of the principle of utility, hereafter referred to as simply "the principle of utility." Accordingly, I shall call an argument for conferring (or denying) a liberty right on (to) a class of persons that considers and balances the happiness and misery of all who would be affected by this an "argument from utility."

It is contended that the principle of utility, correctly applied, would show that we are justified in denying legal A-liberties to children.* This is so for two reasons. First, the objectionable direct effects of paternalistic restrictions on adult liberty do not occur when legal A-liberties are denied to children. Second, the side effects of restricting the liberty of children are on balance good. I shall consider both of these points in turn and conclude with a discussion of the principle of utility itself.

*It is also contended that the principle of utility could be used to justify granting legal C-claims for children. The argument is roughly the same as that presented below for the claim that it is justifiable to deny them legal A-liberties, namely, that both the direct effects and the side effects of granting children legal C-claims are on balance good. Limitations of space prevent me from presenting the full argument. See chapter 10 for utilitarian considerations relevant to a particular legal C-claim of children.

Direct Effects of Paternalism

Direct effects of paternalistic restrictions on liberty are those that relate solely to the person(s) whose freedom of action is restricted. John Stuart Mill provided the most forceful statement of the objection to paternalistic restrictions on *adult* liberty by asking us to consider the bad direct effects of such restrictions. He held that an attempt to restrict the liberty of action of an individual for his own good is likely to produce more harm than the harm it is introduced to avoid. Specifically, the harms that Mill had in mind were to the interests of all persons in their growth and self-realization. "Self-realization consists in the actualization of certain powers and abilities."[1] In order to accomplish this, one must constantly practice at making difficult choices: "The human faculties of perception, judgment, discriminative feeling, mental activity, and even moral preference are exercised only in making a choice. He who does anything because it is the custom makes no choice. He gains no practice either in discerning or in desiring what is best. The mental and moral, like the muscular, powers are improved only in being used."[2]

Since freedom of choice is necessary to the attainment of self-realization, it follows that granting rights to liberty to competent, fully informed adults would have the tendency to promote the good of the people who are given the liberty, even if this freedom permits them to make dangerous or foolish mistakes. It follows, then, that the most that the state is justified in doing when there is substantial risk and the individual is capable of rational choice is to *educate* people to the existence and nature of the risk, or even temporarily to *enjoin* them in order to make certain that their subsequent choice is "calm and cool," but never to *coerce* them from choosing the risky course of action altogether.

On the other hand, Mill would argue, if we remove the legal barrier to a child's exercise of the choice to perform a potentially self-harmful action this would only reveal a *natural* obstacle in the form of that child's lack of capacity to make a rational choice. Mill does not use the latter phrase. Instead, he writes of children not being "in the maturity of their faculties." But his point is clear: children are not yet "capable of being improved by free and equal discussion."[3] As such, it would be useless to educate or inform children about the existence or nature of a risk involved in their conduct, and it is doubtful anyway that children would stand to gain anything (by way of developing character or intellect) that would offset the potential for harm that is inherent in many of the choices that the law now denies to them.

These considerations call for the following version of the argument from utility for denying legal A-liberties to children:

(1a) Unless denied legal A-liberties, children are (i) likely to do harm to themselves or to fail to promote their own good. Moreover, (ii) they cannot be educated about the risks involved in pursuing certain courses of conduct, and (iii) these restrictions on their freedom will not interfere with their growth or process of self-realization.

(1b) It is morally justifiable to deny legal A-liberties to a class of persons if: (i) members of that class are likely to do harm to themselves or to fail to promote their own good unless denied that right, (ii) they cannot be educated about the risks involved in pursuing certain courses of conduct, and (iii) these restrictions on their freedom will not interfere with their growth or process of self-realization.

From premises (1a) and (1b) we derive:

(1c) It is morally justifiable to deny legal A-liberties to children.

What lies behind premise (1a) is the dubious assumption that children are not "in the maturity of their faculties." I believe that there has been sufficient discussion of this in the preceding chapter to cast doubt on it, at least if it is intended to apply to all or most persons legally classified as children. But even if we grant this assumption, Mill must contend with an empirical point stressed in the argument from potential moral agency: we maximize children's chances of developing into fully autonomous or self-determining beings by placing upon them more and more responsibility for their choices from an early age. Hence, it is claimed that statement (iii) of premise (1a) is false.

Mill would probably respond to this by denying the penultimate claim. That is, he would argue that we do *not* maximize children's chances of developing if we place on them more and more responsibility for their choices from an early age *beyond a certain point*. One does not maximize the chances of development if the child gets himself or herself killed or if the responsibility proves too heavy to bear and the child has an emotional breakdown. In short, there are limits, and beyond these limits the balance shifts to the side of misery and legal paternalism is justified.

But what of those persons who are already "in the maturity of their faculties," who have attained the capacity for rational choice? The assumption of statement (iii) of premise (1a) is that restrictions on their freedom *will* interfere with their process of self-realization. Is this true? Some philosophers have doubted that the facts will support this empirical claim. Although it may be true that large-scale restrictions on freedom of action would produce some retardation in the development of the average adult person's intellect or character, it is doubted that this claim can be made about *particular* restrictions, and it is particular restrictions that are our present concern. For example, I doubt that there would be a stunting in the growth of the average adult's process of self-realization if the state decided to deny all persons the legal right to smoke tobacco.

This leads to a third and more extensive criticism. The utilitarian claim is that we maximize children's chances for happiness in the future by legally restricting their liberty now. For example, we think that children will have a greater chance for happiness in the future if they are properly educated than if they are not; hence, we deny them the right to choose for themselves whether to attend school. But can't the same argument be pressed with regard to the adult? Can't it be argued that we *might* maximize *his* chances for happiness in the future by paternalistically restricting his liberty now? Mill would deny this. He would contend that if we restrict competent adults' liberty for their own good, then we reduce their chances for self-realization and so reduce their chances for happiness. But this is to make the dubious assumption that the *only* thing involved in being happy is being self-realized. If we give up this assumption, then it follows that freedom may *not* be the source of happiness. Francis Schrag puts the criticism in this way:

> The growing complexity of civilization, the increasing interdependence of spheres of activity, allows us to envisage a future world in which most adults are like our own children. We say that our children will come to agree that we were acting in their interests when we refuse to allow them to risk their future happiness by remaining unschooled, to take an example. We say that they could not possibly appreciate the consequences twenty years hence of entering the world uneducated. But can we not imagine farsighted individuals able to recognize that much that we do now is not merely injurious to others and to future generations but shortsighted in just the same way—that in twenty years, we ourselves, will profoundly regret the choices we have made, choices, for example in the areas of diet or resource conservation or family planning. If maximizing the chances for happiness in the future is the test, such farsighted individuals would be justified in restraining us in our own interest.[4]

The preceding two criticisms of the argument for premise (1c) come together in the following way. First, even if the results of an empirical investigation show that competent adults would not have their process of self-realization affected by paternalistic restrictions on their liberty, we would still not think the restrictions justifiable. Second, this result is not avoided by giving up the assumption that all that is involved in happiness is self-realization, for the criticism is more general. It is that maximizing one's chances for happiness is not the test of a justifiable restriction on liberty. We would balk at agreeing to paternalistic legislation restricting liberty even if convinced that this would maximize happiness. Hence, the principle of utility, applied in premise (1b), does not help us to articulate why we do not always agree to paternalistic legislation.* I conclude, then, that premise (1b) cannot serve as the complete justification for denying rights to liberty to persons, including children.

Side Effects of Paternalism

Direct objections to paternalistic restrictions on liberty are designed to show that children do *not* suffer from having their liberty restricted and, indeed, that such restrictions may increase their long-range chances for happiness. Side effect objections, on the other hand, are designed to show that by giving liberty to children*persons other than the children* will suffer. Thus, even if the children are made unhappy by placing legal restrictions on their liberty, other persons may be made happy by this, and it is the balance of happiness over misery of *all* persons affected that is to dictate whether children's freedom of action is to be restricted.

People have interests, and they are made happy by having these interests satisfied. There are a variety of interests (other than those of children) that must be considered in deciding whether or not to grant liberty rights to children. Thus, there are the interests of parents. Their interests might be no more than to satisfy certain basic desires, such as those for love, warmth, companionship, importance, power, or protectiveness. One can imagine how some of these desires would be frustrated if certain liberty rights were granted to children. For example, it might be argued that a female child, granted the right to arrange for an abortion without having to obtain parental consent, is legally permitted to do something that harms the interest that her parents have in maintaining power or control over her life.†

*The Kantian tradition in ethics would have no difficulty in explaining why this is so. If we ought to respect people's autonomy, then the decision should be theirs, even if there are no direct, beneficial effects of making the decision (e.g., self-realization). See chapter 4.

†The "family harmony" argument was rejected by the Supreme Court in its decision in *Planned Parenthood of Central Missouri* v. *Danforth*, 428 U.S. 52 (1976). Justice Blackmun, who delivered the majority opinion, had stipulated that "safeguarding the family unit and parental authority" are indeed goods that the state should attempt to promote. However, he argued that it may sometimes be counterproductive to the ultimate goal of promoting family harmony to refuse to accord children certain legal rights, as in the case at hand, the right of a pregnant minor to obtain an abortion without parental consent: "It is difficult . . . to conclude that providing a parent with absolute power to overrule a determination, made by the physician and his minor patient, to terminate the patient's pregnancy will

Finally, there are the interests of the entire community. In order to give an account of the community's interest we must "take into account the ideal of the good life its members share for its interest will lie not only in perpetuating itself as it exists but in making it possible for future generations to come closer to that ideal."[5] Thus, a community might be collectively committed to the ideal of self-determination, where members of the community are encouraged to work out their own ways of life in response to their own assessments of current conditions and their own interests, needs, and capacities. This sort of community would obviously put a greater value on granting legal rights to liberty to its children than would a community collectively committed to the social ideal of, say, securing the minimal conditions for living or maximizing each person's own expectations for satisfaction.[6]

Since there are several parties whose interests would be affected by granting (or denying) rights to liberty to children, the utilitarian legislator must not only clearly identify whether the respective interest is better protected by granting or denying the legal right in question, but he must also weigh the interests of each party against the others. The latter could prove to be an insuperable task, for he must try to preserve those elements of the good life that he believes have already been realized while at the same time evaluating existing arrangements in the light of the sketchy and probably incoherent conception of the social ideal to which members of the community are collectively committed.

The Principle of Utility

The preceding objection is practical, and though it is a problem for any attempt to apply precisely the utilitarian principle to the question of liberty rights, such objections are not fatal to utilitarianism as an approximate guide to how one is to answer such questions. My next objection, however,

---

serve to strengthen the family unit. Neither is it likely that such veto power will enhance parental authority or control where the minor and the nonconsenting parent are so fundamentally in conflict and the very existence of the pregnancy already has fractured the family structure" (ibid., at 75).

I would add to this the observation that the motive of a parent in providing for his or her children may have nothing to do with a desire for power or the maintenance of authority over the child. It may be, and often is, love for the child. There is no basic incompatability between parental love and a child's exercise of a legal right to liberty. A parent who is legally unable to veto a decision of his or her child to have an abortion may believe that the child is mistaken, but if the bond of parental union with the child is love, then this bond will remain intact even when the child has acted in defiance of a parental order to do otherwise.

is moral, that is, it is the objection that the principle of utility would lead us to advocate morally objectionable restrictions on liberty.

The example is familiar to those acquainted with discussions of utilitarianism: suppose there is a society where there are a few slaves in proportion to the free community, and it seems that the majority of society is happier under this arrangement than if the slaves are freed. That is, although the slaves suffer by having their liberty restricted, most people in the society are made happy by this arrangement, so that the balance of happiness over misery is greater than if society foregoes their happiness by freeing the slaves. We would, however, be likely to find this social arrangement morally repugnant, on the grounds that it is *unjust*. It therefore seems that we judge such situations not only in terms of the balance of happiness over misery but also in terms of the way in which the happiness is distributed. We may "prefer a situation where it is reasonably equally distributed to one where the total of benefit is higher but the disparities between the best off and the worst off are great."[7]

John Stuart Mill attempts to refute this objection by both admitting the need for a principle of just distribution and attempting to show that the principle of utility in fact incorporates it: "That principle is a mere form of words . . . unless one person's happiness, supposed equal in degree . . . is counted for exactly as much as another's. Those conditions being supplied, Bentham's dictum, 'everybody to count for one and nobody for more than one,' might be written under the principle of utility as an explanatory commentary."[8]

It is not clear what Mill means. If he is saying that when we do our calculations, we must make sure that we take account of the happiness or misery of all persons affected by our action, then this is compatible with inequality in distribution. On the other hand, if he is saying that the principle of utility enjoins us to promote the greatest good *of the greatest number*, then this affirms the preceding objection. "If we understand it thus, the principle does tell us that we are to distribute a given quantity of good to more people rather than fewer, when we have a choice. The principle of utility thus becomes a double principle . . . it has become a combination of the principle of utility with a principle of justice, and to read it thus is to give up pure utilitarianism."[9] It follows that there is not just one basic principle of morality, that of utility, which tells us to maximize the total amount of good or happiness in the world, but another independent principle, not "incorporated" into utility, which tells us how the good is to be distributed.*

*This is not to suggest that the battle is over. Jan Narveson finds the preceding criticism of utilitarianism to be "seriously misleading." His argument is that the objection wrongly assumes that we have an obligation to distribute happiness equally. However, he argues, we

Conclusion

The argument from utility tells us that we are justified in denying to children legal A-liberties because: (1) the "direct effect" objections to paternalistic restrictions on adult liberty do not apply to children, and (2) the "side effects" (on persons other than children) of restricting the liberty of children are on balance good.

I have set aside my earlier point that both premise (1) and premise (2) assume an erroneous conception of (most) children as beings who lack the capacity for rational choice. I have instead concentrated in this chapter on the normative assumptions of each argument. First, I have shown that since premise (1) assumes that liberty is valued only because it is a means to the happiness of the person who possesses it, then the "direct effect" objections to paternalistic restrictions on adult liberty cannot be made. If they cannot be made with respect to the question of adult liberty rights, then the fact (if it is a fact) that children are not on balance made unhappy by having their liberty paternalistically restricted cannot be the (complete) justification for such restrictions.

Second, I have argued that the fact that denying certain adult liberty rights to children produces beneficial side effects does not provide a complete justification for denying these rights to children. If it did provide a complete justification, then we are committed to the view that whenever the side effects of restricting a person's liberty are on balance good, we are justified in restricting his liberty. However, as I have shown, this view has morally objectionable results (as in the slavery case). Hence, legal restrictions on liberty are not completely justified by side effects. It follows that we cannot use this principle alone in an argument designed to show that we are justified in denying legal A-liberties to children.

A final note. I have been discussing the hedonist version of the principle of utility in this chapter. As noted earlier, this is the version that holds that "good" means happiness and "bad" or "evil" means misery. However, I would hold that the preceding criticisms hold for *any* version of the

---

have no obligation to distribute anything; *a fortiori,* we have no obligation in general to distribute anything equally (*Morality and Utility* [Baltimore: The Johns Hopkins University Press, 1967], p. 206). Narveson may be right that most of us have no obligation to distribute anything. But surely there are *some* of us who may have an obligation to distribute *some* things equally. Thus, if I am a legislator who has to distribute legal liberty rights, then I have a duty to distribute these equally. (In chapter 8, I try to clarify the notion of equal distribution.) It is this that lies behind the traditional counterexample to utilitarianism, the utilitarian case for slavery cited earlier. We think that slavery is *unjust* and we think this precisely because we think that legal liberty rights have been *unequally* distributed by those who had the duty to distribute them.

principle of utility, hedonist and nonhedonist alike. Thus, my argument that good side effects do not alone justify restrictions on liberty would hold even if, say, we interpret the notion of "good" to mean knowledge and "bad" to mean ignorance. The point is that one can always imagine a morally objectionable restriction on liberty dictated by a "good" side effect.

7 *The Argument from the Social Contract*

In my introductory remarks to chapter 5 I made the point that teleological arguments for denying legal A-liberties to children share the view that a being has a right to X if and only if the state ought to defend him in the possession of it, all things considered. This is to make rights derivative from more general moral principles and to reject the view of the argument from moral agency that moral rights are somehow morally basic (that is, not derived from general moral principles).

There is another argument for denying legal A-liberties to children that shares the preceding view. I call it "the argument from the social contract." Although it agrees that rights are to be derived from more general moral principles, it does *not* agree that the only rights it is morally reasonable to enforce are those we can derive from *teleological* principles. Instead, it insists that the rights that are to be enforced are those that a group of ideally rational beings would be compelled (by the power of their rationality) to choose if they came together to pick rules to govern their mutual relations.[1]

This interpretation of rights is basic to the social contract theory elaborated by Professor John Rawls in his renowned book *A Theory of Justice,*[2] and it is the interpretation I shall use in this chapter. The book is very complex and the argument detailed and elaborate. Since my aim is to show what Rawls says (or would say) about the problem of granting legal rights to children, what follows is only the minimum account required to make those remarks intelligible.

The Justification of Principles of Justice

First, there is what Rawls terms the *Main Idea*. This is the claim that any moral principle (or social practice) is rationally justified if that principle (or practice) would be agreed to, adopted, or contracted for by a group of free and rational persons coming together in what Rawls calls the "original position," in order to pick principles and practices to govern their forms of social life and institutions. The "original position" is a hypothetical situation in which men and women with ordinary tastes, talents, ambitions, and convictions unite to form a social contract. What distinguishes their congress from those imagined in the classical social contract theories is that these people are temporarily ignorant of the aforementioned features of their personality, and they must agree upon a contract before their self-awareness returns. They operate under what Rawls refers to as a "veil of ignorance." They know, in general, what can happen to persons in various positions in society but do not know what their own position is likely to be. Finally, the people in this hypothetical assembly are *self-interested*, that is, primarily concerned to promote their own welfare (and the welfare of those about whom they care deeply), and they value a set of "primary goods." These are "things that every rational man is presumed to want. These goods normally have a use whatever a person's rational plan of life." The primary goods can be either social (such as self-respect, liberty, wealth) or natural (such as health and vigor, intelligence and imagination).

As mentioned above, Rawls intends his theory of the original position as a justificatory device, that is, he wants the choice of principles by persons in the original position to constitute a justification of them. For example, Rawls attempts to show that the principle of utility is *not* justified because it *would not* be chosen by rational persons in the original position. Since utilitarianism allows for such practices as slavery if this results in substantial benefit to the majority, it would never be unanimously agreed to by persons in the original position. Rational agents, caring most about protecting such primary goods as liberty and having no guarantee (because of the veil of ignorance) that they will not be members of the enslaved class, will not choose a principle that allows this practice.

In their condition of ignorance and self-interest, the parties in the original position would choose two fundamental principles of justice. The first of these is immediately relevant to the current discussion, and it runs as follows:

> Each person is to have an equal right to the most extensive total system of equal basic liberties compatible with a similar system of liberty for all. . . .
>
> Liberty can be restricted only for the sake of liberty. There are two cases: (a) a less extensive liberty must strengthen the total system of liberty shared by all; (b) a less than equal liberty must be acceptable to those with the lesser liberty.[3]

The basic liberties to which Rawls refers are not merely what I have been calling "rights to liberty." They include the right to vote and be eligible for public office; freedom of speech and of assembly; liberty of conscience and freedom of thought; freedom of the person, along with the right to hold personal property; and freedom from arbitrary arrest and seizure. Although Rawls does not explicitly mention it, he would probably also include other important forms of liberty, such as sexual freedom and the liberty to use alcohol or drugs, even though they do not fall within any of the aforementioned "basic" liberties.

Rawls has another principle that is especially relevant to the issue of granting legal C-claims to children.* However, space limitations require that I defer comment on it until chapter 10, where I discuss it in connection with the general topic of child neglect. My focus in what remains of this chapter, as in the preceding chapter, is on the justification for denying legal A-liberties to children.

The Social Contract and Paternalism

What are the implications of Rawls's first principle of justice (quoted above) for children? Are we to restrict their liberty only if we can prove that this secures a greater or more extensive liberty for all or if we first obtain their consent to a less than equal liberty? If so, then it would appear that Rawls would grant the same rights to liberty to children that he would grant to competent adults. Prohibiting children from voting or holding public

*The principle is this:
"Social and economic inequalities are to be arranged so that they are both:
(a) to the greatest benefit of the least advantaged, consistent with the just savings principle, and
(b) attached to offices and positions open to all under conditions of fair equality of opportunity" (John Rawls, *A Theory of Justice* [Cambridge, Mass.: Harvard University Press, 1971], p. 221).

There is not sufficient space here to make clear precisely what this principle involves. Suffice it to say that since children and not competent adults are granted legal C-claims, there are (ipso facto) social inequalities that exist between these classes of persons. However, Rawls would probably argue that these inequalities satisfy conditions (a) and (b). By granting legal C-claims to children (for example, by granting them the right to an education, to health care, etc.), we insure that children will have as great a chance as competent adults of occupying advantaged positions later in life. That is, their legal C-claims go toward insuring that the chances of children do not depend merely on their own natural endowments or their motivation to succeed. Hence, as Rawls would put it, the social inequalities that now exist between children and competent adults are not "arbitrary."

office would secure no greater or more extensive liberty for all than would be secured if we prohibited competent adult females from voting or holding public office. In either case, Rawls's first principle would not allow the prohibition.

However, Rawls does not come to this extreme libertarian conclusion with respect to granting rights to liberty (or power rights) to children. In the original position, the parties "will want to insure themselves against the possibility that their powers are undeveloped and they cannot rationally advance their interests, as in the case of children."[4] In this case the parties "adopt principles stipulating when others are authorized to act in their behalf and to override their present wishes if necessary; and this they do recognizing that sometimes their capacity to act rationally for their good may fail, or be lacking altogether."[5] Second, the principles that the parties would adopt are "the principles of paternalism." They do this in order "to protect themselves against the weakness and infirmities of their reason and will in society."[6] Third, they would authorize other persons to act in their behalf only on the understanding that these persons do what they would do for themselves if they were rational:

> Paternalistic decisions are to be guided by the individual's own settled preferences and interests insofar as they are not irrational, or failing a knowledge of these, by the theory of primary goods. As we know less and less about a person, we act for him as we would act for ourselves from the standpoint of the original position. We try to get for him the things he presumably wants whatever else he wants. We must be able to argue that with the development or the recovery of his rational powers the individual in question will accept our decision on his behalf and agree with us that we did the best thing for him.[7]

Rawls realizes that the latter requirement that the other person in due course accepts his condition is not sufficient:

> Thus imagine two persons in full possession of their reason and will who affirm different religious or philosophical beliefs; and suppose that there is some psychological process that will convert each to the other's view, despite the fact that the process is imposed on them against their wishes. In due course, let us suppose, both will come to accept conscientiously their new beliefs. We are still not permitted to submit them to this treatment.[8]

The analogy with children is obvious. It is surely possible to socialize and educate a child in such a way that we can almost guarantee that he will later agree to the way in which we restricted his liberty. Suppose, for example, that we deny children the legal right to play at certain games. We then indoctrinate them so that as adults they come to agree that our decision to deny them these rights as children was correct. Clearly, the fact that they are now persuaded of the correctness of the decision does not justify the decision.

Therefore, Rawls makes two further stipulations about paternalistic intervention. It "must be justified by the evident failure or absence of reason and will; and it must be guided by the principles of justice and what is known about the subject's more permanent aims and preferences, or by the account of primary goods."[9] In the case of children the first stipulation is satisfied by definition. As for the second stipulation, children either have no "permanent aims and preferences" or they have them but they cannot "rationally advance" them. Hence, we must guide our intervention "by the account of primary goods." That is, whenever we intervene paternalistically (for their own good) we must take into account the fact that they, like all other persons, can be presumed to want self-respect, liberty, health, and other social or natural primary goods.

Criticisms of the Argument

The following is a rough statement of the social contract argument for denying rights to liberty to children, based on the preceding account:

(1a) Children cannot rationally advance their interests.

(1b) It is morally justifiable to deny legal A-liberties to those who cannot rationally advance their interests if this is done for paternalistic reasons and in accordance with the theory of primary goods.

Therefore,

(1c) It is morally justifiable to deny legal A-liberties to children if this is done for paternalistic reasons and in accordance with the theory of primary goods.

Let us assume for purposes of argument that Rawls does not mean by the word "children" all those who are presently classified by law as "minors" or "infants," that is, he does not mean to include all persons who are under the age of eighteen (or, for some purposes, twenty-one) years in this class. Instead, he means to include only those persons who are clearly unable to "rationally advance their interests," and he expresses no view as to in what age range this lack of ability is present. In this way we can dispense with arguments about whether children do or do not have the capacity for rational choice.

Nonetheless, it is important to note that the social contract argument would probably deny to children (understood as those who cannot rationally advance their interests) the same rights to liberty that would be denied them under the argument from beneficence.* Thus, if any right to liberty is such that if granted to children their exercise of it would probably be harmful to them or would not be conducive to their best interests, then this right must be denied to them (so long as this is done in accordance with the theory of primary goods). However, paternalism is seen by Rawls as an appropriate reason for intervention, not because he sees this as derivable from a more basic moral principle (as it is in the arguments from beneficence and utility), but because persons in the original position would adopt paternalism in deciding what rights to grant to children. That is, premise (1b) in the above argument is ultimately derived from the general justificatory principle that we should grant a right to a class of persons if and only if a law guaranteeing that right would be chosen by rational agents in the original position.

The latter remarks invite two questions about Rawls's endorsement of paternalism: (*a*) why would persons in the original position settle on paternalism as a principle of intervention in the lives of children? (*b*) why should the choice of the principle of paternalism by persons in the original position constitute a justification of it?

Choosing Paternalism. Rawls would answer question *(a)* above by stressing that it is rational and prudent for persons to adopt this principle. One first has to imagine what it would be like to be a child, that is, a person who lacks the capacity for rational choice. We are next to suppose that children, like everyone else, would want such things as health, intelligence, liberty—in short, the items on the list of primary goods. If this is so, then, as another author has suggested, "one could agree that the attainment of such goods should be promoted even when not recognized to be such, at the moment, by the individuals concerned."[10] If a child is likely to engage in a course of action that would endanger his health, then we are justified in interfering, regardless of what he says that he wants, because health is a primary good. In general, persons in the original position would want to be interfered with for paternalistic reasons because, as children,

*The preceding account of the application of Rawls's theory of justice to the normative question of what rights the state ought to accord to children appears to conflict with the account given by Victor L. Worsfold in his article "A Philosophical Justification for Children's Rights," in *The Rights of Children,* ed. Harvard Educational Review (Cambridge, Mass.: Harvard Educational Review, 1974), pp. 29–44. Worsfold claims that Rawls's point of view, while not radical, "seems to contain major implications for children's rights" (ibid., p. 40). It is not clear to me what these implications are, and Worsfold never provides a list of the legal rights (e.g., to liberty) that he thinks can be derived from Rawls's particular brand of paternalism. In my interpretation, Rawls's argument simply defends the status quo.

they would want health, intelligence, liberty, etc., and thus would want to be helped by others in obtaining these goods.

One might object to this answer by arguing that it leads to a paternalism that is more extensive than most of us would think justifiable. If the criterion of paternalistic intervention in the lives of children is that we want them to attain the primary goods, then why restrict such intervention to children? So long as the coercion is in the direction indicated by the primary goods ("what persons in the original position would want"), then even someone who is not a child could be justifiably coerced. At least in principle, it is possible for Rawls to be committed to a paternalistic policy of restricting the liberty of a competent adult, in what are taken to be his own interests but against his expressed wishes.

Rawls might reply to this by arguing that the account of primary goods can be appealed to in the case of paternalistic decisions on behalf of children only either because we do not know what they want or because their preferences and aims are irrational. In the case of a competent adult, however, their aims and wants are usually known or are rational. Hence, it is not justifiable to intervene paternalistically in their (adults) lives.

This reply is unsatisfactory. First, we usually do or can know what most children want. Their case is not analogous to that of an unconscious person about whom we have no personal information and who needs immediate medical attention (such as surgery) in order to save his life. Here, we must assume that he would want surgery on the grounds that this is how "we would act for ourselves from the standpoint of the original position." But children are not unconscious. Unless they are very young, they are capable of expressing (and do express) their wants, aims, and preferences.

It follows that the burden of Rawls's case for paternalistic intervention in the lives of children must rest on the point that their choices are (usually) "irrational." It is not entirely clear what Rawls means by this term, but let us suppose that he would accept one of the applications of this term suggested in chapter 5: a choice is not rational if it puts the chooser in a situation in which his life or bodily integrity is at risk. But on this interpretation of "not rational," we may still press the earlier criticism of Rawls's case for paternalism in the lives of children, namely, that it may allow us to justify paternalistic intervention in the lives of competent adults as well. To repeat Francis Schrag's point, in a complex technological society such as ours there are areas (proper diet, resource conservation, family planning) in which most of us are simply unable to make a rational choice.[11] Even granting that there are far-sighted individuals who are able to recognize that much that we now choose to do in these areas we will come to regret profoundly in, say, twenty years, we would resist any suggestion that such individuals would be justified in restraining us in our own interest. It is not clear that Rawls's theory of paternalism could justify this resistance.

The Justification of Moral Principles. The second question posed above is much more difficult for Rawls to answer, and several authors have suggested that the problems Rawls would have in answering it signals the downfall of the contract theory, or at least exposes a serious weakness in it that must be remedied.[12] Rawls believes that it is fair to require people to submit to procedures and institutions only if, given the opportunity, they could in some sense have agreed in advance on the principles to which they must submit. This is an important point to remember when legislators turn to the task of deciding what rights to give or deny to children. They must do their work such that when children attain the capacity to reason they will see that had they been in the same position of choosing principles they would have agreed to the ones actually chosen. But this hypothetical agreement does not justify the principles chosen. It is not the fact that persons in the original position would adopt them that justifies the principles chosen. Actual or possible prior agreement does not sanction anything. What we want to know is *why* they chose the principles in question.

Since the parties in the original position must arrive at a unanimous choice, Rawls assumes that the theory of primary social goods is a sufficient basis for parties to act on when choosing a moral principle. Recall that the parties do not know their full conception of the good but only know that income, wealth, power, and self-respect, for example, are desirable, whatever else they want or desire. This eliminates other conceptions of the good (such as peace, security, good reputation, honor), because if they were allowed, no unanimity in principles would result. However, as Thomas Nagel has argued, it is one thing to rule out morally irrelevant grounds like race, sex, parentage, or natural endowments, but it is quite another to deprive persons in the original position of knowledge of their particular conception of the good. The latter are certainly not "morally irrelevant":

> If someone favors certain principles because of his conception of the good, he will not be seeking special advantages for himself so long as he does not know who in the society he is. Rather he will be opting for principles that advance the good for everyone, as defined by that conception. (I assume a conception of the good is just that, and not simply a system of tastes or preferences.) Yet Rawls appears to believe that it would be as unfair to permit people to press for the realization of

their conception of the good as to permit them to press for the advantage of their social class.[13]

Nagel's point is that Rawls must suppress information that is morally relevant if he is going to achieve unanimity among the parties in the original position. But this means suppressing it in a way that does not treat the parties equally. The primary goods will serve to advance many different individual life plans (some more efficiently than others), but "they are less useful in implementing views that hold a good life to be readily achievable only in certain well-defined types of social structure, or only in a society that works concertedly for the realization of certain higher human capacities and the suppression of baser ones, or only given certain types of economic relations among men."[14] If I have a conception of the good that depends heavily on the relation between my position and that of others (for instance, honor), and this knowledge of the good is to be suppressed, then it is suppressed in a way that is unfair. "Why should parties in the original position be prepared to commit themselves to principles that may frustrate or contravene their deepest convictions, just because they are deprived of the knowledge of those convictions?" I conclude, then, that because the original position treats parties in it unequally and unfairly, the choice of principles by parties in it cannot justify our adopting these principles.*

*Indeed, as Nagel goes on to point out, it can be argued that the original position *must* treat parties in it unfairly. For if we were to redesign the original position to do away with the restrictive assumption, then "either the parties would retain their conceptions of the good and, choosing from different points of view, would not reach unanimity, or else they would possess no aims of their own and would be asked to choose in terms of the aims of all the people they might be—an unintelligible request which provides no basis for a unified choice, in the absence of a dominant conception" ("Rawls on Justice," in *Reading Rawls: Critical Studies on Rawls' A Theory of Justice*, ed. Norman Daniels [New York: Basic Books, 1976], p. 10).

Part 3
A Theory of Juvenile Rights

8 Outline of a Theory

One approach to the discovery of an argument that will justify the practice of treating *some* children differently from the way in which competent adults are treated under law is to construct an argument that will justify the practice of treating beings who lack the capacity for rational choice differently from competent adults (beings who have the capacity for rational choice). If this can be done, then by showing that some children (for example, children below a certain age) belong to the class of beings who lack the capacity for rational choice, we shall have a justification for this difference in legal treatment. By "difference in legal treatment," I mean to refer to the practice of denying legal A-liberties and granting legal C-claims to children but not to adults.

One difficulty with some of the theories considered in part 2 that attempted to construct an argument along these lines is that they prove too much. Thus, the arguments from beneficence, utility, and the social contract not only show that beings who lack the capacity for rational choice ought to be denied legal A-liberties, but the normative principle employed in each argument can be used to deny many of the very same rights to competent adults as well. The only argument that does not suffer from this difficulty is the argument from moral agency. Instead, this argument proves too little. By restricting the class of beings who possess moral rights to those who possess an autonomous will, it fails to offer a justification for the practice of granting legal C-claims to children.

And yet each argument seems to say something that is important, something that we must attend to when considering the problem of conferring legal rights. Thus, the arguments from utility and beneficence seem to me right in suggesting that one of the things that we ought to consider in deciding what laws to adopt, what rights to confer or deny, is the balance of happiness over misery that we thereby produce. It is difficult to conceive of a morality that allowed one to decide such questions independent of a concern about the existence and incidence of human happiness and misery. Second, the argument from moral agency presupposes that decisions about legal rights have something to do with moral rights. Consider, for example, the firm belief that denying liberty rights to competent adults for paternalistic reasons is wrong at least partly because it violates the moral right to have one's autonomy respected. It matters not *why* we think we have this right; all that is presently important is that we do think this. We have a strong desire to make our own decisions, to run our own lives, and we are prepared to forego a great deal of happiness, or risk a fair amount of disaster, rather than to lose this control of our lives.[1]

Is there a middle path that we may take, an approach that will lead us neither to deny particular rights (liberties) to those beings who we believe ought to possess them (competent adults) nor to grant them to beings whom we normally think ought not to have them (beings who lack the capacity for rational choice)? I think that there is. The clue to the discovery of an argument is to be found by reflecting again on the discussion of the argument from utility. The way in which I characterized the central problem encountered by that argument was that the principle of utility it employed could conceivably lead to *unjust* distributions of legal liberty rights, and so could not alone serve as a basis of denying such rights to beings who lack the capacity for rational choice. What I wish to suggest, then, is that we *combine* the principle of utility with a principle of just distribution in order to avoid this objectionable result. That is, I wish to suggest the following premise as part of an argument designed to justify denying certain legal A-liberties and granting certain legal C-claims to beings who lack the capacity for rational choice:

(1a) It is justifiable to deny a legal liberty right or to grant a claim right to a class of beings if this produces maximum happiness consistent with the principle of just distribution.

Thus, if it can be shown that by denying a particular legal A-liberty or granting a particular C-claim to a class of beings who lack the capacity for rational choice *in fact* produces maximum happiness in a way that is consistent with the principle of just distribution, then we will have justified denying them that right. That is, if we can prove that (for example)

(1b) To deny to beings who lack the capacity for rational choice the liberty right to purchase and/or consume alcoholic beverages is to produce the maximum happiness consistent with the principles of just distribution

then we shall have proved that it is justifiable to deny such beings the liberty right to purchase and/or consume alcoholic beverages.

Moreover, if it can be empirically proven that

(1c) Children below the age of X years lack the capacity for rational choice, then we shall have shown that it is justifiable to deny this liberty right to this particular age group of children.

The crucial premise in the preceding argument is statement (1a). I believe that it retains the best features of some of the arguments discussed in part 2, although I cannot convincingly establish this until after further description of the principle of justice it employs. Suffice it to say now that premise (1a) meets the requirement that laws restricting liberty or granting claims must have some bearing on the increase of happiness or the decrease of misery if they are to be justifiable. Second, the concept of justice used in statement (1a) captures the belief that what makes it wrong paternalistically to restrict the liberty of a competent adult is that it violates an important moral right (the right to respect for one's autonomy). For to say that a moral right has been violated is often something we express by saying that we have been treated unjustly. However, this latter point needs further discussion if I am to establish that there is a rational basis for the intuition that there is a close connection between justice and moral rights.

There are two questions that initially arise with respect to premise (1a). First, what criteria are we to use in deciding when a particular distribution of legal rights is just or unjust? Second, on the basis of these criteria, is it just to discriminate between beings who lack the capacity for rational choice and those who possess it in distributing legal liberty and claim rights?

The Concept of Justice in Distribution

It has often been pointed out that the principle of justice in distribution (or the principle of distributive justice) is in fact two principles: a formal principle and a material principle.[2] The formal principle states that like cases are to be treated alike and different cases are to be treated differently. The material principle supplements this by stating criteria for determining the relevance of likenesses and differences. Now the context that is my present concern is that of lawmaking. Laws or general rules are unjust "when they discriminate between classes that are actually alike in a respect that is 'really and truly' relevant and fail to discriminate between classes that are actually different in a respect that is 'really and truly' relevant."[3] The important question to be answered, then, is what *standard* of relevant differences and likenesses is employed when a particular distribution is said to be unjust?

The answer to this question is sometimes provided by merely attending to the relevance of the features of the class of persons discriminated against to the agreed-upon objectives of the particular law. Consider, for example, the law that prohibits children under a certain age (for example, sixteen years) from obtaining automobile driver's licenses. Why do some people think that this law is just, whereas they would not think it just to deny driver's licenses to (say) all blonde females? That is, why are they sure that being under the age of sixteen years is relevant to the question of being allowed a driver's license whereas hair color and sex are not? The answer must appeal to "the object which the law in question is admittedly designed to realize."[4] The object of laws regulating driver's licenses is to prevent automobile accidents and thus protect the health, lives, and property of motorists, passengers, and pedestrians. It is believed (and insurance companies contend they can prove) that there is a causal connection between age and the risk of being involved in an automobile accident, whereas there is no meaningful statistical connection between hair color or sex and risk. Legal discriminations based on hair color and sex are, therefore, unjust, whereas discriminations on the basis of age are not.

However, I doubt that we can assess the justice of most of the laws denying rights to liberty to children by attending to the relevance of being a child to the object or purpose of the particular law.* This is because the objective of most of these laws is paternalistic, that is, to protect the child from doing harm to himself or to guide the child toward his own good, and it is this *purpose* that is itself to be assessed as just or unjust.

Consider, for example, the law that prohibits child labor. We may agree that being a child is relevant to the objective of the law, for the law is

*But see H. L. A. Hart for an attempt to show that laws that exclude children, or the insane, from the franchise, or withhold from them the power to make wills or contracts, "are regarded as just because such persons lack the capacity, which sane adults are presumed to have, to make a rational use of these facilities" (*The Concept of Law* [Oxford: Oxford University Press, 1961]). I doubt, however, that this has anything to do with "the object which the law in question is designed to realize." Thus, the object of the wills law is to give private individuals the power to see to it that their possessions are distributed to certain designated persons after their death. Surely, this object or purpose would not be generally thwarted by extending to children the right to make a will. The point is not that the purpose would not be realized, but that some children might will items to certain individuals or organizations that they might not have willed were they older. It is, then, paternalism that is the ultimate reason for withholding from them the power to make wills, and (as I try to show below) we must assess the justice of this particular *purpose*.

straightforwardly concerned with the protection of children. Instead, to ask whether such a law is just is to ask whether it is just to behave paternalistically toward children (by denying them the right to work) but not toward adults. A proper answer to this question would involve a lengthy critical discussion of the many possible replies that have been made over the past two thousand years, such as the theses that the basis of just distribution should be wealth, property, merit, or some other feature in which people are thought to be unequal (for example, sex, or race). Instead, I shall offer *one* reply, a theory that I contend provides a defensible criterion of relevance for the just distribution of legal liberty and claim rights.

I propose, then, William Frankena's suggestion that a distribution of something, P, is just if and only if P is so distributed that everyone has an equal chance of achieving the best life he is capable of.[5] This principle is *equalitarian* in that it says that basically P is to be distributed equally to all human beings. Being human is the criterion of relevance for purposes of distributing anything whatever, including legal rights. If P is a legal liberty or claim right and Q is the characteristic of being human, then P is to be distributed in proportion to Q. But since all human beings hold Q equally, it follows that P must be equally distributed among them.

To say "P is to be distributed equally among human beings" is not to say something fundamentally different from what is contained in Frankena's definition of just distribution. In order to see this, consider the fact that the basic standard of distributive justice is *equality* of treatment. Now in order to treat people equally we are not required to give the *same amount* of what is to be distributed to everyone. For example, if I must distribute food among a group of hungry people, I do not treat them equally if I give the same amounts to those who are malnourished and those who are not. To treat them equally requires that I *proportion* my help to their needs. But in proportioning my help to a person's needs I am in effect trying to distribute the food so that "everyone has an equal chance of achieving the best life he is capable of." Doing this may entail giving what seems to be extra attention to certain sorts of people, but, as Frankena remarks:

> Such attention seems extra only because it involves more effort or money, but it is not really extra (unjust), since it is necessary if we are to make the same *proportionate* contribution to the best of life of everyone. Some people simply are by nature harder to help on their way, and others easier, and we are, therefore, not unjust if we put more effort or money into helping some than we do into helping others, as long as all are enabled to make the same *relative* advance toward the good life.[6]

I adopt, then, the equalitarian theory of just distribution, and this is to be understood as the theory that a thing is to be distributed so that everyone has an equal chance of achieving the best life he is capable of. It follows that the relevant features of people we are to attend to when distributing a thing cannot be such features as color, sex, and the like, but "only those features that bear, directly or indirectly, on the goodness or badness of the lives of which they are capable." This is not to deny that being black or being female in our society has a great deal to do with the goodness or badness of one's life. But this is the result of a social system that many think to be fundamentally unjust. That is, one's life is not made good or bad *merely* by being black or being female. It is made good or bad by being black or being female *in a society* that deprives persons who possess such features of equal chances or equal opportunity. Perhaps I should say, then, that the relevant features of individuals to which justice requires us to attend in distribution are those that bear on the goodness or badness of people's lives, *independent of social circumstances*. Thus, independent of how people respond to R, being black has no causal relationship to the goodness or badness of R's life.*

What features of a person do have a causal relationship to the goodness or badness of his or her life? The obvious and oft-repeated answer is: needs and abilities. If someone has a need for something (food, clothing, or shelter, for instance) then his life will be made worse if he does not get it. That is why justice requires us to give special attention to handicapped persons. They have needs that normal persons do not have and so require proportionally more of the (beneficial) thing that is being distributed. That is also why, if a particular burden is to be distributed, proportionately more of the burden is shouldered by those who have special abilities.

Distributing Liberty and Claim Rights

The problem of this chapter is to discover whether it is just to grant legal C-claims to *some* children but not to adults *and* to grant legal A-liberties to adults but not to children. Is this distribution of legal rights just? My

*This point can be easily misunderstood. By the phrases "independent of social circumstances" and "has no causal relationship" I do not mean that one aspect of distributive justice involves rectifying unjust distributions that arise from social circumstances; nor, therefore, do I mean that one might have to pay attention to social circumstances in order to rectify these injustices. Indeed, so much is consistent with my point that a person's needs are to be considered in making just distributions: for the needs may have arisen *because* of prior social circumstances. Instead, what I mean to assert is that a person's color or sex does not *alone* make his life good or bad. The point here is the same as that made by equalitarians against various kinds of meritarian theories.

argument will be that the notion of *need* as a standard of relevance for just (equal) distribution furnishes the clue to an answer.

First, let me restrict the class of children under discussion to those who clearly "lack the capacity for rational choice," as measured against the prudential standard discussed in chapter 5. What, then, would be the argument for the claim that it is just to grant a particular C-claim to this class? On the basis of the preceding considerations it may be said that those who lack this capacity have a particular sort of need (a handicap) that prevents them from having an equal chance with others of enjoying a good life. If left to depend on their own (limited) cognitive and emotional resources, most of them would be unable to provide for their own nutritional, medical, educational, and other "basic" needs and thus either would not survive at all or if they did survive would not have as great a chance as competent adults now have of occupying advantaged positions later in life. Hence, it is justifiable to grant particular legal C-claims to some children and to withhold them from competent adults.

The case for denying legal A-liberties to some children while granting them to adults follows the same pattern. Thus, we are justified in restricting the liberty of some children by denying them legal A-liberties because this provides them with a benefit of protection and guidance, a benefit that uniquely attends to their special needs and helps them achieve the best lives they are capable of. For example, we may deny some children the liberty right to choose their own place of residence, not in order to impose a *burden* on them, but to provide them with a *benefit* of preventing them from exercising this right in ways that would be harmful. It is, therefore, not unjust to restrict the liberty of such children because, having a greater initial burden or deficit (the burden of being unable to make choices that do not put them at risk of doing themselves harm), this brings them up to the same level enjoyed by others.

It is important to see that I have tied the characteristic of capacity for rational choice to need in order to show how an equalitarian can justifiably attend to the former in distributing a liberty right. I have *not* claimed that the capacity for rational choice is a characteristic possessed by some persons justifying their *unequal* treatment. That would be to adopt an inequalitarian principle of distributive justice. Instead, I have argued that when we deny a liberty right to a being who lacks the capacity for rational choice for paternalistic purposes we are in fact according equal treatment to such beings. To repeat: by attending to their special need we are bringing them up to the same proportionate level as their fellows.

This analysis solves a dilemma that sometimes arises for those who compare the legal treatment of children with what is commonly thought to be the unjust treatment of persons on grounds of race or sex. Thus, it is often said that we reject being black or being female as relevant features justifying differences in treatment because people do not have a fair opportunity to avoid or acquire these features. A person cannot help or avoid being a particular color or sex; thus, it is unjust to use these features to justify differences in distribution. But (so the argument goes) it is for this reason also unfair to make *age* a relevant characteristic of a person justifying differences in treatment. A person does not have a fair opportunity to avoid this difference. A child cannot be held responsible for being six years old any more than a black person can avoid being black. Hence, it is argued, it must either be unjust to make legal discriminations on the basis of chronological age or we must reject the fair opportunity requirement. Although some would happily adopt the former, most would be inclined to say that either alternative is unacceptable.

The solution of the preceding dilemma involves the theory of justice adopted above. It is true that a person cannot be held responsible for being the age that he is, but it does not follow from this that it is always unjust to discriminate on the basis of age when distributing legal rights. This is because the age of at least some persons (namely, the very young) is a good indicator of a feature that *is* relevant for purposes of distribution, namely, the lack of capacity for rational choice. Hence, we do not always treat children under a certain age unjustly when we deny them certain liberty rights that we accord to others, for they are not being *unequally* treated by being denied such rights. By attending to their lack of capacity for rational choice, we are attending to their peculiar needs and, as argued above, this is actually a requirement of the principle of equalitarian justice. It was the belief that age discrimination, like discrimination on the basis of race or sex, always leads to unequal treatment that was the source of the dilemma.

Conclusion

At the outset of this chapter I suggested in statement (1a) that we use two moral principles in deciding whether it is justifiable to deny or grant a legal right to a class of beings: the principle of utility and the principle of just distribution. The former principle requires that we maximize happiness and the latter requires that we distribute rights so that everyone has an equal chance of achieving the best life he or she is capable of. Second, I have shown that the practice of denying a particular liberty right to the class of beings who lack the capacity for rational choice while granting this right to the class of competent adults is a practice that can be shown to be consistent with the preceding principle of just distribution. Third, although premise (1a) makes it justifiable paternalistically to restrict the liberty of beings who lack the capacity for rational choice, we cannot conclude from this that it is justifiable paternalistically to restrict the liberty of all children, for (as stressed in chapter 5), we have no empirical evidence that all (or even most) children lack the capacity for rational choice. It follows that unless it can be shown that there is some other relevant respect in which those children who *possess* the capacity for rational choice differ from competent adults, it is unjust (and therefore unjustifiable) to deny to them the liberty rights that the law commonly grants to competent adults. Finally, what I have said about equalitarian justice shows the close connection between justice and moral rights. If I say that (*a*) I have been treated unjustly by being denied a liberty right on paternalistic grounds, then another way of voicing my protest is to say that (*b*) my moral right to have my autonomy respected, to make my own decisions, has been violated. Now the case for making statement (*a*) is to show that I have received unequal treatment, and I would prove this by establishing that there is no relevant respect in which I differ from others: since I have the capacity for rational choice, I have no special need for paternalistic protection. But the case for making statement (*b*) is precisely the same. The moral right to have one's autonomy respected is violated whenever a person *who is capable of making a rational choice* is not allowed to decide for himself what to do. That is, possession of the capacity for rational choice underscores both the case for making statement (*a*) and the case for making statement (*b*). If one lacked this capacity, then he could neither protest that he had been treated unequally by being denied a liberty right on paternalistic grounds nor protest that his moral right to have his autonomy respected had been violated. It is in this way that the concept of distributive justice employed in premise (1a) captures the intuitive belief that an important moral right is violated whenever paternalistic restrictions are imposed on the conduct of competent adults.

9 Goods and Needs

To summarize the theory so far developed, I have argued that we are to use two moral principles in deciding whether to deny a legal liberty right or to grant a legal claim right to a class of persons. First, we should employ the principle of utility. This requires us to calculate and balance the total amount of happiness and misery created by denying or granting a particular legal right to the class in question. Second, we should employ the principle of equalitarian justice, which requires us to compare the treatment accorded the class in question with that accorded other classes. The object is to determine whether members of the former class are receiving treatment that is equal to that accorded members of the latter classes.

There are several gaps in the preceding account. First, I have assumed for purposes of argument that what makes something good is happiness and what makes something bad or evil is misery—the *hedonist* version of the principle of utility. It is now necessary to show why this is a plausible assumption and how the principle of utility can be made more specific for purposes of application to particular cases. Second, the principle of utility does not provide one with any guidelines for weighing the good or bad things that are produced or prevented by laws that grant or deny legal rights. I must, therefore, supplement the principle by such guidelines if the rational legislator is to act on it in any sensible manner. Third, the concept of "need" that plays such a crucial role in the principle of equalitarian justice must be clarified and its use in the application of that principle specified in some detail if I am to avoid some rather obvious objections (noted below) to my adoption of the principle.

Happiness, Goods, and Interests

Many contemporary ethicists have expressed doubt over our ever-reaching agreement on a particular theory of *intrinsic* value, that is, a theory about the sorts of things that are good in and of themselves.* My inclination is to skirt this controversy entirely and simply construct a list of good things independent of settling on a particular theory of intrinsic goodness. I would place on the list only those things that all of us desire, whatever else we desire—a list of "primary goods," as Rawls refers to it.[1] This is undoubtedly less satisfactory than the approach from the standpoint of pure theory, but since theories of intrinsic value are ultimately tested by their coherence with what a free, informed, clear-headed, and impartial person would choose as good, this approach to the problem of discovering what things are good may not be so defective after all. Moreover, even if I cannot get everyone to agree that the only thing that is intrinsically good is happiness, I would claim for the list I provide below that the items that appear on it are things that are *extrinsically* good (that is, good because they are a means to an end that is good) under any plausible theory of value, including (especially) the hedonistic theory I used in the preceding chapter. This is surely all that is needed to allow the discussion to proceed.

What things are we to place on our list? I want to take a hint from the law and construct a list of good things from the *interests* that are legally recognized or protected in most modern legal systems. When legal writers use the word *interest* it is clear that what they mean by this term is that which is "truly good for a person whether he desires it or not."[2] Now I have already classified interests into categories of legally protectable *rights*. Thus, rights to liberty and powers protect our interests in freedom of movement and in self-determination or autonomy. Rights to security protect a person's interest in the safety and security of person and property, reputation, and privacy. Positive rights promote a person's interest in

*One of the main problems appears to be that there is no decision procedure generally agreed upon by ethicists. Thus, some philosophers ("cognitivists") argue that we are to prove basic judgments of intrinsic value by discovering the property denoted by the words *good* and *bad*. Others ("noncognitivists") tell us that these words do not stand for properties; hence, there is nothing to "discover," and no way to prove basic judgments of intrinsic value.

William Frankena has suggested that although we cannot prove basic judgments to be of intrinsic value in any strict sense of proof, "this does not mean that we cannot justify them or reasonably claim them to be justified." He suggests that we do this by taking "the evaluative point of view . . . and then trying to see what judgment we are led to make when we do so, considering the thing in question wholly on the basis of its intrinsic character, not its consequences or conditions." To take the nonmorally evaluative point of view, he writes, "is to be free, informed, clear-headed, impartial, willing to universalize" when one considers such items as pleasure, knowledge, and love. "If one considers an item in this reflective way and comes out in favor of it, one is rationally justified in judging it to be intrinsically good" (*Ethics*, 2nd ed. [Englewood Cliffs, N.J.: Prentice-Hall, 1973], p. 111). I am inclined to side with Frankena in this dispute, and the approach I adopt in this chapter reflects this decision—although I use Frankena's approach to argue for a list of primary goods and not for a theory of intrinsic value.

bodily and psychological health and in receiving a certain amount of education. All of these are "important" interests in the sense that the law deems them worthy of legal recognition and/or protection. I shall assume that in making this judgment, it has done so on the basis that all free, informed, clear-headed, and impartial persons would choose these items—that is, these things are good in the sense that all such persons would desire them, whatever else they desire.

Corresponding to this list of goods is a list of things that are bad or evil. An evil is to be defined as a harm to or an invasion of an interest. Hence, being deprived of sufficient food for subsistence is an evil: a person's interest in bodily health has been harmed. A restriction on or interference with one's freedom of action is an evil: this is a harmful invasion of an interest in autonomy.

There are undoubtedly other items that would appear on a list of things that are good, and in some cases there will be strong disagreement over whether the proposed item *really is good*. Consider, for example, the controversy over the question of whether pornographic material intended for adult consumption ought to be available to children, or the dispute over whether children ought to be allowed to associate with certain "undesirable" persons, such as prostitutes, gamblers, and felons. One form of this controversy is whether a child has an interest in the state of his moral character, his dispositions or tendencies to do certain kinds of action in certain kinds of situations and to think or feel in certain ways. Most would agree that a child does have this sort of interest, that it is rational to want a morally good character. That a child's character be developed or formed in a particular way is surely as important as, for example, the child's interest in privacy, reputation, or capacity for autonomous choice. Whether we can reach agreement on what *particular* virtues or state of the child's moral dispositions is to be cultivated is, of course, another matter. My own view, consistent with the theory I have developed in this book, is that a morally good character is one disposed toward promoting the good of others (benevolence) and treating them equally (justice). Hence, I would find an invasion of a child's interest in the state of his character if, for example, his parent were to train him in the fine arts of cruelty and torture. On the other hand, I see no logical incompatability between a child's being disposed toward certain kinds of (consensual) sexual activity and these virtues of character. Although I realize that there is bound to be continuing controversy on the question of what particular set of virtues or state of character is a protectable interest in children, I have no doubt that there are *some* virtues that everyone can agree ought to be included (for instance, benevolence and justice). In those areas where there is controversy (chastity, for one) I would counsel a great deal of caution in asserting these as protectable interests, for the simple reason that where there is substantial controversy over such evaluative questions, any attempt by the state to "protect" the disputed interest by coercive law is bound to produce evils that outweigh any good that is accomplished.

A second and perhaps more common kind of controversy is over a *causal connection* alleged to exist between the behavior to be restricted and the harm to be avoided or the good to be promoted. The debate over making repeated association with "undesirable" persons a juvenile status offense may serve as an example. All disputants in this debate may agree that a child has a fundamental interest in becoming a certain kind of person (for example, one who is benevolent and just), but they may strongly disagree over the question of whether associating with persons who display antithetical character traits has the effect of producing similar traits in children.

Third, there will be inevitable clashes between the *relative weights* of interests. Consider, for example, the conflicts between the interest in autonomy and the interest in security of person. Is it more important that children be free to act as they choose or that they be secure from bodily harm? Juvenile curfew statutes seem to reflect a legislative choice for the priority of the latter interest. Again, is it more important that children be free to act as they choose or that *other* persons be secure from the bodily harm that a child might inflict on them as an unintended result of his or her exercise of freedom? The laws restricting a child's freedom to obtain an automobile driver's license again reflects a legislative choice for the priority of the latter good.[3]

The most difficult problem of weighing and balancing interests is that of weighing the interests of children against the interests of their parents or other would-be custodians. This is most vividly illustrated in legislative, judicial, and executive child placement decisions concerned with establishing, administering, or rearranging parent-child relationships. The traditional standard used by decision makers is "the best interests of the child." The problem with the standard is that it "has come to mean something less than what is in the child's best interest."[4] Instead of dictating that only the good of the child is to be considered, it has in actual practice been used to *balance* the interests of the child against competing adult interests, with the former often being made subordinate to the latter. Part of the reason for this is that many decision makers assume that children have no interests distinct from those of their parents. This, of course, is absurd—if a parent chooses to assert his interest in autonomy by beating his child, we would not maintain that the child must have an interest in being abused. The real question that is disguised by the "best interests of the child" standard, then, is whether the child's interest in such matters as, for instance, his psychological well-being outweighs the interest of the biological parent in being his custodian. The two may be equivalent, that is, it may be the case that both interests may be promoted by placing the child with her or his biological parent, but we cannot assume that this is always the case. Which interest has the greater weight? I can offer no formula, but the following suggestion may be helpful in particular contexts. If it is clear that the child will be psychologically harmed by being placed with a particular adult (for example, a biological parent), then this may be of greater relative importance than the harm inflicted on the adult by being deprived of the custodianship of the child. For the harm to the child may affect not only his present psychological health but the entire course of his psychological development. This, in turn, may affect his own capability to become an adequate parent for his future children. However, the harm to the adult will often take the form of unhappiness, and although this may be quite intense, it is unlikely to have serious and lasting consequences.

Weighing Interests: Principles of "Practicality"

I propose no formula to answer the preceding questions about the relative value to be placed on competing interests. However, there are two considerations to which I would have an "ideal legislator" attend in balancing a child's interest in liberty against other competing goods. In both cases, the "practicality" of a particular legislative response is at issue.

In the preceding chapter, I argued that the principle of equalitarian justice specifies that we treat people equally only when we attend to their needs. I shall have more to say about the concept of "need" in the next section. But for now, let us suppose that some children, because of their lack of capacity for rational (reasonable) choice, have a need for protection from harm—harm that they might cause to themselves or harm that they might suffer at the hands of others. For example, a legislator, in deciding whether or not to enact a juvenile curfew statute, might be convinced that younger children have a need to be protected from harm that they might suffer at the hands of others when in public places during certain late night and early morning hours. There are at least two conceivable legislative responses that he might make to this acknowledged need: either legally to prohibit children from being in those places (by enacting a juvenile curfew statute) or to give children adequate police protection when they are in public places. What response ought the legislator to recommend? I suspect that the reason that most legislative bodies do not opt for the latter alternative is that it is "impractical." The principle that seems to dictate this choice may be worded as follows: when justice requires that we respond to the need(s) of a class of persons and the only practical way of doing this is to restrict their liberty, then we are justified in restricting their liberty. The problem I have in accepting this principle is due to the ambiguity of the word "practical." It sometimes means "effective," and when it means this I am sympathetic with the legislator who claims that even a greatly enlarged police force would not be adequate to protect children at night in a large metropolitan area. However, I suspect that "practical" is usually construed to mean "less costly," and the choice that the legislator is asked to make is between asking constituents to pay higher taxes in order to strengthen the community police force and the far less costly alternative of enacting a juvenile curfew statute. It is not surprising that the average (nonideal) legislator will vote for the latter alternative. The ideal legislator, unencumbered by the need to please voters, can ask which of these alternatives is the greater evil. Attention to the following consideration might be helpful in arriving at an answer to this question. If the class of children affected by the statute is restricted to those who clearly need the benefit of protection it provides, then the freedom to travel in or to public places unaccompanied by a parent or legal guardian during the specified hours *may* be relatively unimportant. If this is true, then in this sort of limited circumstance, economic considerations may receive a higher priority in making the legislative decision.

There is a "practicality principle" that is also involved when considerations of social utility are at issue. Thus, one might ask whether it would be more practical to satisfy the desire of the public for "safety and order" by adopting a juvenile curfew statute or by strengthening the community police force in order to combat the perceived threat of an increase of juvenile crime. Consider the following principle: when social utility dictates a legislative response to legitimate community interests (such as the security of persons and property) and the only practical way of accomplishing this is legally to restrict liberty, then we are justified in legally restricting liberty. This is surely an unacceptably broad principle! It would justify not only juvenile curfew statutes but general curfew statutes as well—statutes that would restrict the freedom of travel of everyone during whatever hours of the day or night the authorities believe there to be a risk of crime. The reason that the principle allows us to reach this result lies with the phrase "restrict liberty." The phrase does not specify *how much* freedom of action is to be restricted. For example, we deal with the threat to our bodily security that is posed to all of us by those who are prone to acts of violence *not* by requiring everyone to remain locked in his or her home but by prohibiting acts of violence. That is, we choose the narrower restriction on freedom of action consistent with the agreed upon end of bodily security. Hence, we should amend the preceding principle in the following way: when social utility dictates a legislative response to legitimate community interests and the only practical way of accomplishing this is legally to restrict liberty, then we are justified in doing so, *provided that we adopt the least restrictive alternative among those effective*. As an illustration, consider again juvenile curfew statutes. Since there are narrower restrictions on liberty of action that the state can and does impose on children in order to accomplish its purpose of preventing juvenile crime—namely, those restrictions found in the existing criminal laws—it follows that it is not justifiable to adopt a curfew statute, for that statute imposes a wider restriction on liberty in an attempt to achieve the same purpose.

Needs and Justice

The third major gap in the proposed theory of juvenile rights is the lack of definition of the concept of "need" as this notion is employed in applying the principle of equalitarian justice. I have maintained that the need of a person is a morally relevant difference between him or her and others when questions arise about the just distribution of a legal right. Its moral relevance is due to the fact that the need of a person is related to his ability to achieve the best life he is capable of achieving. This gives rise to two questions. First, a conceptual question: what is a need? Second, a normative question: what *sort* of need must be met in order to help a person attain "the best life he or she is capable of achieving"?

Means Needs and End Needs. The verb "need" is a three-place predicate.[5] A need statement of the form "X needs Y" always implies a statement of the form "X needs Y to Z." That is, only in virtue of some Z is it intelligible to say that X needs Y. For example, to say "The sick need medical care" implies that there is something, some end or goal (health) in virtue of which medical care is needed. Second, the Z in virtue of which X needs Y usually has the status of an interest, and thus is something such that if Y is not obtained, X will be harmed. For example, since health is an interest of sick people, they will be harmed if they do not obtain medical care; thus, we say they need medical care. Third, a need, like an interest, is not a mere want or desire. An infant may need open heart surgery to correct a heart defect, but he neither wants nor does not want the surgery. Fourth, some needs are "basic" or fundamental"; others are not. A need is basic if the harm caused to the person whose need is not met is serious or substantial. Thus, my need for an electric typewriter is not a basic need, but my need for food is, for if the latter (but not the former) need goes unmet, this may result in bodily harm or death. Fifth, some needs are such that a person cannot, through his own efforts, meet them. If he is not capable of fulfilling his needs, then we would (somewhat confusedly) say that he has a need for help in fulfilling his needs. If he is capable of fulfilling his needs, then we (even more confusedly) say that he has no need for help in fulfilling his needs. For example, I may need adequate food in order to promote my interest in bodily health, but since I am capable of obtaining my own food, I would deny that I need the aid of others in obtaining it. I shall call the former kind of need an "end need," and the latter a "means need." As I shall show in a moment, the distinction is important.

The kind of need to which we are to attend in applying the principle of equalitarian justice is, in fact, two: a means need to the fulfillment of an end need. Consider the following illustration. In distributing welfare funds we are presumably to attend to the need of different claimants for relief. In deciding whether some particular distribution of funds is fair or just, we must show that the claimants who are given the funds: (1) are actually being harmed in the sense that an interest of theirs is being invaded (for example, an interest in health); (2) this harm can best be avoided by providing them with food, shelter, clothing, or the funds to obtain these (that is, they have end needs); and (3) they cannot provide these things through their own efforts (that is, they have means needs). If any of these conditions is not met, then I would suggest that the distribution of funds is unjust. That is, if it is false to contend either that the persons to whom the funds were distributed have basic end needs or that they have the relevant means needs, then they cannot prove the (overall) need that is a prerequisite for a just distribution of the benefits.

Let me now apply this analysis to a particular liberty right. Consider, again, the legislation that creates juvenile curfew statutes. In deciding whether it is just to deny children the right to be abroad during certain hours while according this right to adults, we must establish that children are being treated equally.* If they are receiving equal treatment, then there is a need of children to which this legislation is a suitable response. Using the preceding set of distinctions, the rational legislator must show that: (1) children are or can be harmed in the sense that an interest of theirs is or will be invaded (in this case, the interest is their bodily health); (2) this harm can be avoided by refraining from specific conduct (being in public places during the specified hours); and (3) they cannot avoid the harm through their own efforts (that is, they are unable to refrain from this conduct on their own). If one could establish either that children do not have the end need specified in statement (2) or that they do not have the means need specified in statement (3), then he will have established that the denial of this specific right to liberty is unjust. One way of showing the latter is to rebut the assumption that the law now makes that all persons under the age of eighteen lack the capacity for rational choice. It is, of course, on this assumption that the law responds to the means need stipulated in statement (3) by denying children the liberty right denied by juvenile curfew statutes.†

End Needs and the Good Life. I have argued that we must attend to a person's end needs and means needs both in order to apply the principle of equalitarian justice properly. However, there are two sorts of end needs: those that are "basic" (that is, those that if not met are likely to lead to serious harm, or harm to an important interest) and those that are not basic. An example of a basic need is the need for food; an example of a nonbasic need is my need for an electric typewriter. The question I must raise here is whether both of these kinds of needs must be met in order to make a just or fair distribution of legal rights.

Justice requires that we attend to *any* need that, if not met, will prevent a person from attaining "the best life that he or she is capable of achieving." The trouble with this formula is that it forces us to answer the question What is the best life that people are capable of achieving? and this in turn means that we adopt some theory of the good upon which we can decide whether or not a particular life is good or bad. That is, the problem is once again the problem I confronted in the initial section of this chapter: what makes a thing good or bad? Only in this case, the thing I am talking about is a

*This is not to deny that others have a need to be protected from the sort of harm that might be caused to them by children who are abroad at night. Hence, they too have a claim for equal treatment. The point I am making in this paragraph is that it may also be just *to children* to deprive them of this particular liberty right.

† The question whether it is "practical" to so respond was discussed in the preceding section.

kind of life instead of a kind of activity or experience. But the problem in providing an answer is the same. Since theories of the good are so many and so varied, there is little hope that we can obtain agreement on any particular theory. However, in connection with my discussion of activities and experiences, I argued that most of us would agree on a particular list of things that are good ("interests"), things that we would want or desire whatever else we want or desire. I think that the same thing can be said about "the good life." Thus, it seems to me plausible to say that the good life is *at least* a life in which one's basic needs are met, for this seems to me to be a prerequisite for our achieving any other kind of life that we believe to be good. Where there is hunger, cold, fatigue, or ignorance, one rarely finds the pursuit of wisdom, honor, or prudence. In this respect, the basic need for freedom from constraint may be especially important, for without freedom we are unable to achieve other acknowledged values that have autonomy as their precondition, in particular, dignity, self-esteem, and responsibility.[6]

However, the good life is not usually thought to be merely a life in which one's basic needs are met. Some would argue that, in addition, the good life is one in which a person engages in primarily intellectual pursuits. Others may choose a life of honor, a life of pursuit of physical pleasure, or a life in which there is a maximum degree of autonomy, "doing your own thing," or creativity. Accordingly, they would argue that a just legal system would meet the needs of persons as determined by the respective conceptions of the good life. This is best illustrated by the decisions that people make in raising children. If people decide, say, that the best life is one of primarily intellectual pursuits, then they will want to give their children the maximum opportunity to actualize whatever potential they have for engaging in such pursuits. Hence, they would argue, what children need is the sort of individualized education that is necessary to help them maximize their intellectual potential.

But why should one assume that the best life for children is the intellectual life? A child may have a gift for higher mathematics, but there are many people who, adopting different conceptions of the good life, would ignore or minimize intellectual potential. My point in raising this question is to indicate that there are great differences in schemes for the good life and the respective differences in what people would say are a child's end needs, beyond and above the initial agreement about "basic" end needs. To opt for any one of these schemes in making a distribution of legal rights would be to force that scheme on parents who may not accept the presumption that their child has a need for the thing they are told by the law to provide. What occurs, then, is a clash of children's needs and parents' interests: the alleged (nonbasic) need of the children versus the asserted interest of the parents in raising their children according to their (the parents') conception of the good life. The risk that we run in demanding that parents provide their children with things consistent with a conception of the good life that is controversial and alien to them is that this reduces them to guardians for the status quo, perpetuating that conception of the good life currently accepted by most middle-class Americans, and thus deprives them of the special rewards that they expect in raising their children according to their own conceptions. I conclude that although justice requires that the state respond to the end needs of children as this is dictated by a conception of the good life, that conception must be limited for purposes of distribution to a *minimum* conception, a conception that commands universal (or nearly universal) assent. The only one I can discover is that life in which a child's basic needs are met.

Justice and Paternalism

The theory as so far developed is limited in two ways. First, it has only been shown to apply to one kind of legal right: rights to liberty. I have yet to show how the theory can be employed to justify the practice of granting or denying other kinds of (Hohfeldian) rights to children, for example, positive rights, rights to security, rights to due process, powers, privileges, and immunities. Second, insofar as I have talked about the just distribution of liberty rights, I have limited myself to an explanation of why it is just to respond *paternalistically* to a particular class of children (those who lack the capacity for reasonable choice, given a prudential standard of reasonableness). However, if the freedom of action of children is legally restricted on grounds other than paternalism, it is important to ask whether this is ever allowed under the restrictions imposed by the principle of equalitarian justice. Neither question poses insurmountable problems. In succeeding chapters (part 4) I will have the opportunity to show that the theory so far developed is quite adequate to help us make decisions about some of the other kinds of legal rights.

The second question can be briefly treated here. It is undeniably the case that most of the laws restricting freedom of action of children are rarely justified on the single ground that the law will prevent the children from doing harm to themselves or will guide them toward their own good. A further justification frequently given is that this restriction on children's liberty will serve the good of all. For example, one justifies denying to children under the age of sixteen years the right to obtain a license to drive an automobile partly on the ground that this will reduce the risk to everyone of being involved in an automobile accident. Hence, this restriction on liberty is morally required by the principle of utility. However, in addition to considerations of utility, our theory also requires that we ask whether the legal restriction on liberty is *just*, and this means that we must ask whether all persons have been or are being accorded equal treatment. There are two ways to interpret this. I have already suggested in chapter 8 that one interpretation demands that we consider the relevance of being under the age of sixteen years to the avowed purpose of the law. Looked at in this way, there is a causal connection between the former factor and the likelihood of being involved in an automobile accident. Given this connection, we conclude that the law is just. However, there is a second interpretation. We might ask whether the avowed purpose of the law is *itself* just. When considering paternalism, our question was Is the paternalistic purpose of a law restricting the freedom of action of a child just? But in the present context our question, Is it just to restrict the freedom of action of a class of persons on the sole ground that they are more likely to cause accidental harm to others if left unrestricted than are members of another class? That is, Is the factor of being more prone accidentally to harm others a difference that justifies unequal treatment under the law?

I would suggest that there is nothing in the principle of equalitarian justice that will allow us to answer this question in the affirmative. However, I don't think that this should trouble us. It seems to me that we commonly accept restrictions on our liberty as a trade-off for protection from harm. We might object that this is unjust, but in this case considerations of utility override the claims of justice. As William Frankena has remarked, "It is tempting to say that the principle of justice always takes precedence,"[7] but, as he goes on to argue, we shouldn't always lean over backward to avoid committing a small injustice.

There is no fixed rule that will show us how to solve the problem of possible conflict between the moral principles of justice and utility. However, the following two observations may be encouraging. First, the principle of the least restrictive alternative enunciated above requires that we restrict liberty in the narrowest manner possible that is consistent with achieving the desired social good. Second, we will rarely find ourselves in the position of having to defend a restriction on the liberty of a child on the *sole* ground that this will promote the good of others. Usually paternalism, that is, thinking of the child's own good, is a prime consideration, and when it is, we have the opportunity to determine whether the restriction on his or her liberty is just, given the consideration of need dictated by the principle of equalitarian justice. If legally restricting liberty answers a clearly determined means need of the child, then both utility and justice may, without conflict, point to the same legal restriction.

Part 4
Applications of the Theory

10 *Status Offenses*

In this (concluding) part of the book my object is to put the normative theory developed in part 3 to the test by applying it to different kinds of legal rights. This will not only serve to clarify and illustrate the theory, but this will actually give it a crucial test of application by showing that the moral principles that comprise the theory are sufficiently specific to allow me to make recommendations about granting or withholding certain legal rights to or from children.

In this chapter I apply the theory to a number of liberty rights, the liberties denied to children by "status offense" legislation. In succeeding chapters I make recommendations about the (positive) claim rights to be accorded to children under neglect statutes (chapter 11) and the claim right of a juvenile to be rehabilitated (as opposed to punished) for an offense (chapter 12).

Certainly the most controversial liberty-limiting statutes on the books today are those that create "status offenses." As defined in chapter 2, a status offense is an offense that only a person who has the status of juvenile can commit. The behavior is troublesome in terms of parental, school, or other authority, but it falls short of violating any criminal law. Under the category of "status offense" are included such acts as truancy, incorrigibility (ungovernability, unruliness, wayward behavior, etc.), smoking, drinking, using vulgar language, violating juvenile curfew laws, consensual sexual behavior, loitering around bars, or associating with felons or gamblers.

Review of the Current Debate

There are four main lines of justification for laws making the aforementioned kinds of conduct illegal for children. First, although the relevant behavior is not as "serious" as the behavior made illegal by the criminal law, it is behavior that is troublesome to parents, teachers, and other authorities. Parents especially may need legal backing in order to rear their children adequately, to coerce them to behave in ways consistent with their values. Second, in some cases at least, these laws may actually deter children from engaging in acts that are harmful to themselves or to others. Third, since some status offenses frequently are due to or typify problems between the child and the family, this jurisdiction allows the juvenile court to intervene in ways that might provide some relief to these problems. Fourth, children who engage in the acts listed above are more likely than other children to commit more serious deviant (delinquent or criminal) behavior at some future time. By making these acts illegal, the court is empowered to intervene early so that it may treat and rehabilitate these children in order to reduce the likelihood of future deviancy.

Those who argue for the abolition of laws creating status offenses contend either that there is no evidence to support the preceding empirical claims or that there are several evils that this jurisdiction tends to inflict on the child and others. First, and most obviously, the child loses his freedom to engage in certain acts, for instance, to choose his own place of residence or to do any of those acts that constitute disobedience of a parental order. Second, the child is stigmatized by being labeled a "status offender." This is not only psychologically harmful to the child by giving him a poor self-image that may in the future cause him to perform even more serious deviant acts, but he may suffer in other ways as well, such as by being denied jobs, being denied entry into academic programs, or having increased police surveillance. In other words, the evil effects of the stigma are so great that they cannot be outweighed by any rehabilitative good that the court may be able to do for the child (if indeed the deviant act indicates any need for rehabilitation). Third, by making these acts offenses we overburden the juvenile court with cases that comprise no less than one-third and probably close to one-half the workload of America's juvenile courts. The result of this is that the courts have inadequate treatment resources to meet the more serious needs of the delinquent child, the child who *has* committed a criminal offense. Fourth, and of most serious concern, is the fact that the juvenile court all too frequently "draws inaccurate conclusions from the facts presented to it and orders a disposition that has no beneficial effect."[1] This is because the courts are not equipped to deal effectively with the noncriminal behavior of allegedly troubled youth. Because judges lack the necessary expertise in diagnosing difficult behavioral problems and do not have at their disposal the resources to deal with them, the cure is often worse than the disease from which the offender is supposed to be suffering. There is overwhelming evidence that too many of these children are institutionalized, and when placed in institutions are subjected to a waiting period of enforced idleness that is ultimately destructive to the child. They are not only treated like delinquents in these institutions, but they come into constant contact with juveniles who have committed serious delinquent acts. The result, it is claimed, is that they too develop a propensity for future delinquency.

Analysis of the Debate

Many of the facts cited by the opponents of statutes creating status offenses are also questionable. I do not for the moment intend to enter the dispute about the empirical data. Instead, I want to approach the topic by getting somewhat more clear about what it is that is in dispute. Accordingly, my first recommendation is to divide the list of status offenses into the following three groups: (1) *misconduct at home and school*: (*a*) incorrigibility (disobedience of parental authority), (*b*) running away from home, and (*c*) truancy; (2) *morally offensive conduct*: (*a*) consensual sexual behavior, (*b*) use of foul language, and (*c*) associating with "undesirable" persons; (3) *conduct dangerous to self or others*: (*a*) smoking, (*b*) drinking, and (*c*) curfew violations.

I make these divisions in order to indicate that some of the reasons given for making a certain type of conduct a status offense are different from those given for other types. For example, one rationale given for group (1) behavior is that "it provides legal backing to parents who need this in order to adequately rear their children." But this is not a rationale usually given for designating group (2) or (3) offenses.* Again, a justification for making conduct in group (3) into status offenses is that (by definition) this conduct is harmful to the child or to others. This is not a reason usually advanced for the existence of status offenses in group (2).

A rationale that appears to be common to all groups is that the child who engages in the indicated behavior thereby displays the symptoms of an underlying psychological disorder, a disturbance that if left untreated will eventually lead the child to commit more serious deviant acts. Hence, the rationale for all of these offenses is *not* that by making these acts illegal the

*I do not mean to suggest by this that this rationale *cannot* be given for group (2) or (3). My point is that most commentators *do not* cite this rationale for these groups.

legislature somehow hopes to *deter* children from committing them; rather, it is to give the juvenile court the authority to *identify* and *commit* those children who need it to a rehabilitative program of treatment or therapy—and this, of course, is said to redound to the good of the child, the family, and the society to which they belong.

Looked at in this way, we would miss the point of enacting statutes creating status offenses if we were to argue that in many cases the act made illegal is not in fact harmful to the child (for example, those acts specified in group 2). This argument is met by those who defend such statutes by claiming that their focus is not on the act itself but on the fact that the act is *symptomatic* of the underlying psychological condition that is its cause. Moreover, since the child cannot help suffering from this condition, he really cannot help displaying the symptom; hence, it would be to no avail to deter him from committing the act. All that the court can hope to do is to identify the symptom and treat the underlying condition.

The second point I wish to make about the current debate over status offense legislation is that it seems to cover two separate areas of concern. One question being debated is about the justification of this type of law: ought the state to prohibit children from engaging in the acts listed in groups (1)–(3)? Another question is about the particular response the state ought to make to persons who are adjudicated as status offenders: ought the state to detain and incarcerate these children in correctional institutions? Although the second question is quite important, my concern in this chapter is largely with the first question. That is, what I want to ask is whether, in terms of the theory proposed in part 3, it is justifiable for the state to make any or all of the acts listed in groups (1), (2), and (3) illegal for children (and only for children) to perform? I shall deal with the general question of disposition in chapter 12.

Applying the Theory

The two principles that comprise my theory to justify creating and enforcing legal rights are utility and justice. If one asserts that it is justifiable to make illegal any of the acts specified in groups (1), (2), or (3), then in each case the general good is maximized and all persons have received equal treatment. Is the consequent of the preceding conditional true, that is, is it the case that the general good is always maximized and that all persons will have been treated equally?

Status Offenses and the General Good. I suggested in chapter 6 that decisions about the utility of a particular piece of legislation should take into account both the direct effects and the side effects of that legislation. Consider first the rights that the state denies to children by making illegal the acts specified in group (2). If the direct effects of this are beneficial, then the items in group (2) specify important interests of children that would be invaded or harmed unless children were denied the relevant legal liberty rights. This seems questionable. I argued in chapter 9 that although children do indeed have an interest in the state of their moral character, since there is strong disagreement over the question of whether children have an interest in that *particular* state of moral charcter manifested in consensual sex, the use of foul language, or consorting with "undesirable" persons, we should not specify this as a legally protected interest. Moreover, even though I defended the claim that certain states of character are indeed interests (such as the traits of benevolence and justice), it is not clear that even repeated association with people who are "undesirable" in that their behavior does not manifest these traits will invade the child's own interest in developing such traits. If this association becomes a mode of conditioning or "brainwashing" of the child into developing antithetical character traits (for instance, a disposition to be cruel), then we can talk about the invasion of an interest, but not until then.

It is not only doubtful that status offense legislation in group (2) is of any direct benefit to children, but (as mentioned in my introductory remarks) there is a great deal of evidence that the effect of this legislation is on the whole bad. Thus, although the juvenile court is allowed to intervene benevolently whenever a child consorts with undesirables, uses foul language, or engages in consensual sex, the intervention may cause the child to suffer psychological damage from being labeled a "status offender," and this labeling may have future bad effects both on the child (the loss of job opportunities, denial of entry into academic programs, etc.), and on society (the child may come to commit more serious antisocial acts in the future). All of this appears to add up to a utilitarian case *against* creating status offenses of these types.

The case for making it illegal for children to commit the acts mentioned in group (3) is perhaps better than the case for the acts in group (2), but it is still arguable that the amount of good created by status offense legislation in this group outweighs the amount of evil. Nonetheless, the acts listed in group (3) do indicate important interests of a child that can be harmed. If there are *repeated* acts of these types (smoking, drinking, curfew violations), then the interest invaded is that of bodily health or security. Hence, it can be safely asserted that one beneficial direct effect of this legislation may be that it prevents children from doing acts that may be harmful to themselves. And yet at the same time, it may be objected, it gains this benefit only at some cost to the child, the family, and society. The costs are the bad effects of such legislation mentioned in my discussion of group (2) acts in the preceding paragraph.

The acts listed in group (1) also constitute difficult cases for legislative decision on utilitarian grounds. One problem is whether in each case there is a clearly specifiable interest that the child is invading by engaging in one of the acts mentioned in group (1). In the case of the runaway the interest is often the child's physical and psychological health and even freedom. For example, boys and girls who run away from home to large American cities are often easy prey for persons who coerce them to commit illegal acts of drug selling or prostitution, or to act as models or actors in what has now become a lucrative pornographic film industry featuring teen-age and preteen children. Again, the disobedient or unruly and the truant child have yet different interests that are being harmed by their persistent behavior: interests in maintaining a good relationship with one's parent or guardian, and an interest in receiving an adequate education.

What is not clear, however, is that in each of the above cases it is likely that the runaway, disobedient, or truant child will be helped by making this behavior illegal. Once again, what is assumed (but rarely proved) is the causal judgment that legal prohibition will reduce the number of such acts, and the evaluational judgment that children will be better off if they do not engage in such behavior. In each case, the assumption is open to serious objection.

Finally, in reflecting on the general utilitarian case for creating and enforcing status offenses it is important to see that one can build just as strong a case for making most of these acts illegal for adults. Thus, if there are reasons for thinking that children would suffer if granted the liberty right to, say, use foul language, to consort with undesirable persons, to drink, or to smoke, then surely one can use the same considerations to show that adults also suffer by being allowed to exercise these rights. I am inclined to think, therefore, that if there is an argument justifying status offenses for children, it must have something to do with establishing the justice of these laws instead of with their overall utility. I turn now to attempts to justify status offenses by applying the principle of equalitarian justice.

Status Offenses and Justice. If it is just to make children (but not adults) subject to the sort of liberty-restricting laws found in status offense legislation, then it must be established that such laws treat children equally. But if their treatment is equal, then (consistent with the analysis in the preceding chapter) status offense laws in fact respond to a special need of children, a need not possessed by adults. In order to show that children "need" status offense laws, it must be shown both that children have the relevant "end needs" (needs to do or refrain from doing acts that are harmful) and that they have relevant "means needs" (they are unable to avoid doing such acts through their own efforts).

The case for saying that status offense laws respond to the end needs of children has already been stated. It is identical to the case for saying that status offense laws are of direct benefit to children. As noted above, the case for saying this is often weak.

Arguments designed to show that children have means needs are identical to the arguments employed in chapter 5 to prove that children "lack the capacity for rational choice." That is, the evidence for saying that children have a need to be prohibited from committing acts of the sort listed in groups (1)–(3) is simply that without the prohibition they would choose to commit such acts: they do not have the capacity to choose otherwise (to make the "rational" choice).

However, as I argued in chapter 5, the evidence for saying that children lack the capacity for rational choice will only support this claim if it is qualified to the class of very young children. There is no adequate evidence to support the claim if it is intended to include older children (for instance, those over the age of thirteen years). Hence, older children do not have a means need for the sort of legal restraint embodied in status offense legislation, and it is unjust to subject this class of children to such laws. We treat them unequally by restricting their liberty in these ways.

What, then, shall I say about status offense laws directed only toward those children who clearly lack the capacity for rational choice? Although this lack shows that they have a means need, it is difficult to see how status offense laws are an appropriate response to this need. One would assume that such laws serve their purpose by *deterrence*. But if young children lack the capacity for rational choice, then ipso facto they would not be prone to respond to the threat of coercive interference by refraining from committing status offenses. That would be a rational response.

What, then, *is* the purpose of status offense laws if it is not deterrence? The answer to this question, mentioned earlier, is that such laws enable the juvenile court to make early identifications of those children who might in the future commit more serious deviant acts. The child who commits one of the acts in groups (1)–(3) shows such a tendency (psychological disorder). By prohibiting these acts the court is able to identify and interfere in the lives of the children who commit them in order to rehabilitate them and so head off future misbehavior.

The most alarming thing about this argument is that it justifies judicial interference in the lives of children not primarily for what they *have done* but for what they *might in the future do*. The reason that this is seen by many as a just response has to do with the whole purpose of the juvenile court system: to rehabilitate the child. Since the ideology of the system is cure or treatment, it is quite understandable that those who defend the system would not want to wait until the child engages in seriously harmful conduct before attempting to treat his or her psychological disorder. They want to arrest the development of the disorder at the earliest possible stage, and they see this stage as being the point at which the child engages in the acts in groups (1), (2), and (3).

A proper response to this argument would involve an examination of the whole ideology of the juvenile court. I am going to defer this analysis until chapter 12. For now, I will assume the appropriateness of the rehabilitative purpose of the juvenile court. Nonetheless, there seems to be little evidence that there is a connection between committing a status offense and suffering from the sort of psychological disorder that will dispose one to commit even more serious deviant acts in the future. There is a great deal of doubt about both the existence of the "disorder" and the causal connection between the disorder and the tendency toward future deviancy. First, it is not clear that all or even most of the children who commit status offenses suffer from psychological disorders. Some people argue that this behavior is seen as simply "transitional deviance, hardly indicative of a lifelong (or even short term) commitment to criminal behavior." Indeed, the challenge of authority, typical of many status offenders, whether it be that of the parent, school, or other institution is "not only normal in an adolescent but essential in the establishment of his or her personal identity."[2] Second, "as yet no behavior patterns or personality tendencies have been isolated and shown to be the antecedents of delinquency, and it is unlikely that they will be."[3] Thus, it cannot be argued that the acts committed by status offenders are always symptomatic of underlying tendencies that may later cause the child to commit even more serious deviant acts.

Conclusion

I urge the abolition of juvenile status offenses for children who have developed the capacity for rational choice. If empirical evidence shows that children above a certain age are capable of understanding the nature and consequences of acts in groups (1)–(3), and they can restrain themselves from doing them (if they wish), then we can say that they have the capacity for rational choice (see chapter 5). In short, if they have the minimal cognitive and emotional capacities we attribute to adults, it would be an injustice to subject children to different treatment from that received by adults by subjecting them to status offense legislation. Although a strong utilitarian case (establishing that a great amount of good is produced by subjecting children who possess the capacity for rational choice to status offense laws) might justify the state in treating children unequally, I have argued that there is no such case. Indeed, evidence now seems to establish that on balance more evil than good is brought about in our society by creating and enforcing such laws for older juveniles. Hence, they are unjustifiable and ought to be abolished.

The crucial question is whether some or all status offense laws should be retained for those (younger) children who have not as yet developed the capacity for rational choice. I have argued that the purpose of such legislation cannot be that it deters such children from offensive behavior. Rather, it gives the juvenile court a justification for benevolent intervention, the assumption being that children who commit acts in groups (1)–(3) suffer from a psychological disorder that needs to be treated. Although I have rejected the assumption (because many children who engage in these types of conduct may be behaving in an entirely normal or appropriate way),* I have not rejected the notion that it is justifiable for the state to interfere paternalistically in those cases where children have an "end need" (an important interest that they need protected) and a "means need" (they are incapable of protecting this interest by themselves). I have ruled out those acts in group (2) as being "important interests" of children—they are too controversial to be accorded this status—therefore, we are left to decide whether to retain as status offenses those acts in groups (1) and (3). My suggestion is that we retain them but only if we can show that there is an important interest of children that is affected by their engaging in such activity. I suggest that this is not shown unless a child repeatedly performs these acts—*repeated* school truancy, disregard for parental authority, running away from home, or consumption of substances known to be dangerous to health (for example, tobacco products, intoxicating beverages). In any case, I agree with the recent findings of a national task force

*For example, in many cases the runaway child is the victim of serious parental neglect or abuse.

that the juvenile courts should not take jurisdiction over these behaviors until it is clear that the allegations are true and all available and appropriate outside services have been exhausted.*

*For example, in the case of runaway children, the state might provide temporary shelter facilities for them, the staff of which would have the responsibility of notifying the minor's parents of his or her whereabouts and condition, and providing services necessary to find a secure living arrangement for the minor. Cf. National Institute for Juvenile Justice and Delinquency Prevention, *Working Papers of The National Task Force to Develop Standards and Goals for Juvenile Justice and Delinquency Prevention*, vol. 5, *Jurisdiction: Status Offenses: A Comparative Analysis of Standards and State Practices*; 9 vols. (Washington, D.C.: U.S. Department of Justice, 1977), p. 10.

11 Child Neglect

In the preceding chapter I dealt with problems arising from specific denials of liberty rights. Indeed, the theory proposed in part 3 was itself largely developed in terms of liberty rights. It is now time to show that the theory can be applied to nonliberty rights as well. I have chosen for this purpose two sorts of positive claim rights. In this chapter I consider a group of claims that children have under the neglect jurisdiction of the juvenile court. In chapter 12 I examine the claim of delinquent children to a therapeutic or rehabilitative response to their deviant behavior.

Children have the positive legal right to be provided with a proper home, subsistence, medical care, and a proper moral environment. Those who bear the legal duty to provide these things are the parents or legal guardians; if this duty is violated, the parent-child relationship is subject to coercive intervention under the neglect jurisdiction of the juvenile or family court. Another aspect of this jurisdiction under which the court may intervene is a violation by the parents or legal guardians of a child's security right not to be (nonaccidentally) physically injured by them. If the corresponding duty is violated by the parents, then this is referred to as an act of child abuse. The rough distinction between abusing children and neglecting their needs is that in the former case there is a violation of the duty to refrain from doing something *to* the children (for example, physically assaulting them) and in the latter case there is a violation of the duty to do something *for* them (for example, to provide them with adequate food).

In this chapter I limit my discussion to acts of child neglect, and the question I want to ask is What positive claim rights ought to be accorded a child under the neglect jurisdiction of the juvenile court? Although most people would agree that children have the right to the satisfaction of their basic biological needs for food, shelter, clothing, and adequate medical care, the agreement seems to stop here. Some would want to add much more to this list; others would restrict it to these items. Thus, courts have been known to grant neglect petitions on the ground that parents have failed to provide their child with the proper moral environment, proper care, safe home conditions, and satisfaction of emotional needs. Some of these are merely restatements of the failure to provide for one or more of the basic biological needs (failure to provide proper care), but others add a new item to the list (failure to provide a proper moral environment). My question, then, is where to draw the line, and this means that one must suggest criteria for determining when the court may use its neglect jurisdiction to intervene in the parent-child relationship on the basis of a violation of a child's positive rights.

I shall approach this question in the manner adopted in the last chapter. I shall begin by giving a summary sketch of the current debate on the topic, then critically analyze the positions taken by those engaged in the debate, and conclude with my own suggestions based on the theory advanced in part 3.

Review of the Current Debate

In recent literature, the normative question about the positive rights to be accorded a child under the juvenile court's neglect jurisdiction seems to have been obscured by replacing it with another question. That question is whether the statutory bases for coercive state intervention on the basis of child neglect should be defined principally in terms of parental behavior or in terms of specific harms to the child. In order to show why I think that this question "obscures" the more important normative question, let me review the current debate on the problem.

Virtually all present neglect laws focus on parental behavior by employing such terms as "lack of proper parental care" or a parent's "moral unfitness" or "faults or habits." There are two reasons given for this focus. First, children may suffer a wide variety of harms as a result of parental misbehavior, and "these harms cannot be accurately defined in advance of an examination of each case."[1] Hence, it is more appropriate to concentrate on parental behavior than on specific harms. Second, there is sufficient available evidence to allow us to correlate specific harms with specific parental behaviors. "Thus, for example, a parent's drug addiction or mental retardation is per se viewed as a basis for family court jurisdiction on the ground that it provides an index to harm to the child."[2]

The alternative approach to finding suitable bases for court intervention under the neglect jurisdiction stresses that the statutes should be written in terms of specific harms to the child, such as physical injury, emotional damage (for example, severe anxiety, depression), or disease causing substantial impairment of bodily functioning.[3] The argument for this alternative mode of statutory language is essentially an argument *against* the current focus on parental behavior. It is also claimed that the defects of this focus are repaired by dwelling on specific harms. First, to focus on parental behavior is wrongly to assume that there is a correlation between parental behavior or home conditions and some specific detriment to the child. But according to child development specialists there is no such correlation.[4] Second, to intervene solely on the basis of parental behavior is to allow intervention where no harm has yet been done to the child. In the absence of specific harm, the trauma caused to the child by the intervention may in itself be more serious than whatever evils are thought to exist in his or her present situation. Third, we should make a presumption in favor of family autonomy in constructing laws. This requires minimum state intervention. But to focus on parental behavior encourages state intervention on grounds that do not comport with this ideal by allowing officials to intervene because they disapprove of a parent's life style or political, religious, or moral opinions.[5]

Analysis of the Debate

The first two arguments against emphasizing parental behavior in statutory language can be combined in the following way:

(1a) We cannot predict harm to the child by focusing on parental behavior.

(1b) To intervene where we cannot predict harm to the child is often to worsen his or her situation.

(1c) If intervention worsens a child's situation, then we ought not to intervene.

Therefore,

(1d) We ought not to intervene on the basis of parental behavior.

The first premise is certainly false. If the parental behavior in question is, say, failing to provide food, then we can certainly predict harm to the child. Now it may be objected to this counterexample that what is intended by the phrase "parental behavior" in premise (1a) is such behavior as "lack of proper parental care" or behavior that shows that the parent is "morally unfit," and where there is *this* behavior we cannot predict that there will be harm to the child. My response to this objection is that what it shows is that the emphasis is not on parental behavior per se, but on particular *types* of parental behavior. It follows that we can construct neglect statutes using words that refer to parental behavior so long as we are careful to specify only particular types of behavior, namely, those types in which there is a close correlation between engaging in the behavior and causing harm.

Second, we should notice that the unwanted result of worsening a child's situation by coercive judicial intervention in his or her life is not necessarily avoided by switching the focus of statutory language from parental behavior to specific harms. It all depends on the *type* of harm that we are prepared to prevent by law. Harm is the invasion of an interest. There are several different types of interest, some of which we may decide are sufficiently important to protect by law. Suppose we decide that children have an important interest in the state of their moral character, and suppose that the evidence that a child has suffered harm to this interest is provided when the child begins to manifest certain kinds of morally offensive behavior, for instance, he becomes sexually active and uses foul language. Although we have now reverted to the language of specific harm in our statute, I doubt that those who advocate a focus on this form of statutory language would advocate judicial intervention on the basis of evidence of this particular *type* of harm.

Applying the Theory

I have said that an important question has been obscured by this debate between defenders of the parental behavior approach and those who opt for the specific harms approach to the wording of neglect statutes. That question is about the specific claim rights the state ought to accord to children. Settling the question about the form of words to adopt in neglect statutes is not going to answer this question. The only way to answer it is to revert to a rational theory of juvenile rights.

The question of what legal claim rights we ought to grant to children is to be answered by discovering what legal claim rights are indicated by the principles of utility and justice. Let me begin by working out the implications of the latter principle for our question. Justice, or rather equalitarian justice, requires that everyone be treated equally. When this principle is applied to the distribution of legal rights, it means that the distribution must be such that everyone has an equal chance of achieving the best life he or she is capable of achieving. If this is correct, then a society like ours can be condemned as profoundly unjust if it should fail to provide children with at least some of the claim rights that we normally associate with neglect laws. Consider the way in which the *absence* of such rights would affect the life prospects of some children, namely, those whose parents are unwilling to provide for their needs (and who cannot provide for their own needs). Without the legal right to receive adequate nutrition and health care from their parents, for example, their chances of achieving the best life they are capable of achieving would be vastly smaller than the chances of those fortunate enough to be born of parents who are willing to provide these things.

I have also argued (in chapter 8) that in order to achieve this equality of opportunity it is often necessary to proportion the benefit provided by law to the needs of those receiving the benefit. This means in turn that people who have a claim to special treatment: (*a*) have "basic" end needs, and (*b*) cannot fulfill or meet these needs through their own efforts (they have means needs). It follows that if we are to grant children those claim rights normally found in the neglect jurisdiction of the juvenile court, then we must show both that this provides for a basic end need and that children have the relevant means needs.

An end need is "basic" if it is a need for something that, if not met or provided for, causes harm to an important interest. What interests are important? I have said in chapter 9 that this is a question that ultimately forces us to make some sort of decision about the nature of "the good," or "the good life." Since ethicists themselves are in such fundamental conflict over even such matters as how to go about answering this question, I expressed doubt that we could construct here a theory that would command much assent. My suggestion was that instead we settle for a list of things about which we can say *most* persons would want, whatever else they want, for instance, bodily and psychological health. Hence, basic end needs would include such noncontroversial items as enough food and medicine to remain healthy, minimal clothing, housing, and so on. On the other hand, since there is such strong disagreement in our society over such matters as proper sexual behavior, standards of dress and comportment, and the value of leading certain kinds of "lives" (for example, an intellectual life or a life of sensitivity to the feelings of others), we cannot claim any particular view as expressing an important interest. Hence, we cannot plausibly argue that a child has a basic end need for such things as a stimulating intellectual environment, color-coordinated clothing, parents who refrain from extra-marital sexual encounters, and so on. Therefore, I would strongly agree with those commentators who argue that juvenile or family court judges ought not to be allowed to use the neglect jurisdiction to enforce "middle class values."[6] Where this means that judges ought not to intervene coercively on the ground that they find that the child has a need for that particular sort of life style we associate with the American middle class, then there is no justification (via the principle of justice) for the intervention.

We reach the same result if we approach the question from the standpoint of the principle of utility. A consistent utilitarian can only argue against legal recognition (in neglect statutes) of a particular interest on the grounds that it (as a matter of fact) does not maximize the good. This is always a contingent question that may be refuted by the evidence. But the evidence seems to show that the good is not, in fact, maximized by allowing coercive court intervention on bases other than that the child's basic end needs are not being met by his or her parents. There are a number of calculations that must be made to reach this result. We are to consider not only the effect of coercive intervention on the child, but also the effect on the family and on the entire community in order to balance the advantages and disadvantages. If we intervene, say, to save the child from serious physical injury, then our calculation would obviously show that the overall good is maximized by the intervention. The injured child might suffer some psychological trauma by the intervention, and the abusing parents might be made unhappy, but the overall gain for the child and the community would outweigh these disadvantages. Suppose, however, that the court intervenes because it finds that the child is dirty, poorly dressed, and constantly exposed to parental marital infidelity. In this case, the calculation would probably go the other way. The psychological trauma to the child produced by judicial intervention would worsen his or her situation, the parents would suffer, and it is difficult to see how the community would gain at all except in the sense that it would have created a social arrangement in line with its particular conception of ideal family life. I doubt that the latter interest, if it truly exists, is sufficiently important to outweigh the former interests of the child and the parents.

Conclusion

The preceding discussion delineates guidelines for state intervention to protect children whose parents do not provide for them. The guidelines I suggest are based in part on the standard of basic end needs. Intervention is permitted only in cases where a child's basic end needs are not being met.

The *evidence* that these needs are not being met is either that the child *is* suffering harm to an important interest or that he, or she, is *likely* to suffer harm to an important interest. Since we can sometimes predict that a child is likely to suffer harm to an important interest from the fact that the parents are engaging (or failing to engage) in a certain type of behavior or conduct, I cannot rule out statutory language that specifies parental behavior.

Let us consider the basic end need of a child for adequate food, clothing, or shelter. By "adequate" I mean sufficient to prevent substantial impairment of bodily function. I would advocate that the evidence the court should require for intervention is *either* that the child is suffering from substantial impairment of bodily function as a result of failure to provide food, shelter, or clothing, *or* that the child is not receiving adequate food, shelter, or clothing (that is, he is not receiving from his parents the amount or type of food, shelter, or clothing that is known to be sufficient to prevent substantial impairment of bodily function). Notice that in the former case the language is that of "specific harm," whereas in the latter case it is that of "parental behavior."

Although I advocate the standard of basic end needs in constructing guidelines for state intervention on the basis of child neglect, I do not wish to suggest that this will allow us to avoid the central problem in writing the relevant statutory language. The problem is that of formulating a standard for intervention that will not *itself* lead to judicial *overintervention* in family life, thereby causing more harm to children than the harm we intended to prevent. Consider, for example, the question of whether psychological or emotional harm should constitute a basis for juvenile court jurisdiction. I have stated that children have an important interest in psychological health. However, we do not know precisely what this means, and thus we do not know what counts as psychological or emotional harm. First, mental health professionals are certainly not unanimous regarding the definition of mental illness and serious emotional disturbances, although there are some symptoms of serious emotional harm on which most mental health professionals seem to agree (for example, severe anxiety, depression, or withdrawal).[7] Second, we have little empirical evidence about what it is that a child needs in order to prevent emotional harm. A recent influential book contends that children need to be "wanted," that is, they need to feel loved, valued, and wanted by at least one other person.[8] The result of not being wanted takes "the form of the individual's diminished care for the well-being of his own body, or for his physical appearance and clothing, or for his image presented to his fellow beings."[9] In general, what is damaged "is his love and regard for himself, and consequently his capacity to love and care for others."[10] This contention is supported by studies documenting deficits in the psychological development of institutionalized infants (some of whom received excellent physical care). But other studies indicate that we know very little about the relationship between child development and parental behavior—indeed, we know so little that we cannot predict psychological harm to the child from even specifically defined parental behavior.[11] My own conclusion from this is that in lieu of firm evidence that specific parental behavior leads to specific emotional harm, we ought not to specify in neglect statutes what kinds of parental behavior a child needs (basic end needs) in order to avoid the harm; that is, we ought not to impose any specific duties on parents to do things for their children that will prevent psychological damage. The reason, to repeat, is that this would make likely too much intervention in the lives of children, intervention based, for example, on a social worker's or judge's brand of "folk psychology,"[12] and that might in the end cause rather than prevent psychological harm.

What, then, can be done? At present the most we can do is to impose on parents a legal duty to provide mental health care whenever their children exhibit symptoms of serious emotional damage, and we enforce this duty regardless of whether the parent is believed to be at fault for the damage. Hence, I would agree with Professor Michael Wald's suggestion that the relevant section of a neglect statute should be worded so that intervention is allowed only if "the minor is suffering serious emotional damage, evidenced by severe anxiety, depression or withdrawal, or untoward aggressive behavior or hostility toward others, and the parents are unwilling to provide treatment for the child."[13] However, if future evidence from psychological researchers proves that certain types of parental behavior give rise to serious emotional damage, then I would advocate that we immediately change the wording of the statute to reflect this fact.

A final word. Where there are basic needs of children that the state must respond to, it appears to me that coercive intervention in the parent-child relationship is only the last step in a number of options available in order to meet these needs. For example, as a national commission has recently suggested, the United States government should institute "a program to ensure that families have the minimum income necessary to provide adequate food, shelter, and care for children" and a national health insurance program to supply medical care.[14] Although I have not argued here for the position that children ought to be granted the legal right to a program that provides a "welfare floor," this is surely one kind of program that is justifiable in terms of my theory, provided that the "welfare floor" satisfied basic end needs only (that is, did not provide a floor one or more steps above this level.)* One immediate effect of this kind of program is that no parent could reasonably respond to a neglect petition by arguing that he was financially unable to provide for the basic needs of his children.

Second, to make a more radical suggestion, we might (if all else fails) consider requiring parents to obtain certification prior to having children. In order to obtain the certificate a parent must show that he or she has sufficient knowledge about such crucial matters as early childhood nutritional needs and the symptoms of childhood disease. In this way the state can ensure that no parent can reasonably claim ignorance as an excuse for failing to meet the corresponding basic needs of a child. Although there is little or nothing that such programs can do to create parents who care for and love their children, it might at least impress on them the seriousness with which the state regards the decision to bear children. This might, in turn, give some potential parents pause to rethink their decision, and that, in itself, would represent an advance over the situation that exists at present.

*Thus, a program that uses tax monies to provide for the "need" of children for certain kinds of "after school" activities, or summer camps, would go beyond the basic end needs "minimum" level.

12 *Rehabilitation and Justice*

In my discussion of Supreme Court decisions relevant to the rights of children (chapter 3), I remarked that the *Gault* decision did not reach the question of whether there is adequate justification for the practice of treating juvenile offenders separately through a system of specialized courts whose goal is to rehabilitate these children. I, too, avoided this question in my discussion of status offenses (chapter 10). The purpose of the present chapter is to correct this omission by critically examining the rehabilitative purpose of the juvenile court. My aim is to show that the usual criticism that this purpose is not, in fact, realized is only a small part, and a misleading part at that, of a *moral* criticism of this purpose. Although such (utilitarian) considerations might ultimately prompt us to abandon rehabilitation as a general aim of the juvenile court, there are far more important moral considerations to which we must attend in assessing this aim. These are considerations of *justice*, considerations that are fundamentally different from those that prompt us to criticize the court by pointing to its failure to prevent juvenile recidivism. Although it may sound odd, and perhaps perverse, to suggest that we do an injustice to children by categorically subjecting all of them to an institution whose sole aim is to "help" them, I will show that, given the conception of justice adduced in part 3, this charge can be adequately substantiated. I conclude with some general remarks about the features that must characterize a *just* system of social response to juvenile crime.

Preliminary: The Nature and Justification of Rehabilitation

What is rehabilitation? There are several ways of approaching a definition of this term. One approach would have us focus on the *type* of thing done to or for the person who is being rehabilitated, for example, moral education, occupational training, behavior modification or conditioning, psychoanalysis, brain surgery, or sterilization. However, what we want from a definition is not a list of examples of the thing to be defined. We want to know what is common to these examples over and above the fact that all of them are called modes of treatment. Nor will it do to focus on the *person* who performs the therapy and declare that rehabilitation is anything done by a psychologist, physician, or social worker. It is obvious that some of the aforementioned modes of treatment could be used by one of these persons not for the purpose of treatment but for other purposes, such as revenge, experimentation, or a display of technical skill. What these considerations point to is a definition of the concept of rehabilitation in terms of the *purpose* of the persons who engage in the act of therapy. Using this approach, we shall say that rehabilitation is a response to others that is made because of some condition from which they are suffering, with the intention of helping those people by attempting to eliminate or relieve them of that condition.

Why, then, does rehabilitation as a response to social deviancy call for justification? When someone asks for the justification of the practice of punishing people for behaving in socially deviant ways we can easily imagine the point of asking the question. Since punishment involves the imposition of pain or some loss (of life, freedom, rights, or property) that is deliberately imposed on an individual without his or her consent, the problem of justifying this practice seems obvious.[1] With the justification of rehabilitation, matters are otherwise. The immediate reaction to the claim that it requires justification is puzzlement, and the reasons for this are apparent from the very definition of rehabilitation proposed above. With therapy, unlike punishment, we do not seek to deprive people of something acknowledged as a good, but rather to help and to benefit the individual who is suffering by ministering to his illness in the hope that he can be cured. Why, we may ask, does *this* need to be justified?

The answer to this question is to be found by looking to the context in which rehabilitation is employed. The context is that of social deviancy, specifically deviations from the norms imposed on us by criminal law. When rehabilitation is used as a response of the state to this sort of deviancy, then it is normally *coercive*, that is, it involves imposing some loss of liberty on the people who are being rehabilitated without their consent. Although, unlike punishment, the motive for imposing the loss of liberty is not to make the people suffer, but to facilitate their cure, coercing them to submit to the therapy may be integral to it—and it is this, the loss of liberty, that needs to be justified.

The second aspect of rehabilitation that requires us to seek its justification as a response to social deviancy is that some forms of rehabilitation are painful. It is prima facie morally wrong deliberately to inflict pain on people without their consent. Hence, the problem of justification. Third, some forms of therapy involve changes in people made against their will. This is especially inevitable when the illness from which the person is believed to be suffering is "psychological" or "mental" illness. Herbert Morris has remarked that "the evil in this would be most apparent in those cases where the agent, whose action is determined to be a manifestation of some disease, does not regard his action in this way. He believes that what he has done is, in fact, 'right,' but his conception of 'normality' is not the therapeutically accepted one."[2] Clearly, most attempts to change a person so that he functions in a way that we want, or in a way regarded as normal by the current therapeutic community, is something that needs to be justified.

The problem of justifying the practice of rehabilitation is now somewhat narrower. What we want to know is whether the practice of subjecting those who are found to violate criminal law to a system of coercive rehabilitation is justifiable. This question breaks down into three questions that we might otherwise confuse.[3] (*a*) a question of justification: Why should we ever restrict a violator's liberty, cause pain, or attempt to change a personality or character as part of an attempt to rehabilitate or cure a violator? What is the justification of this? (*b*) a question of distribution: Whom should we coercively rehabilitate? and (*c*) questions of manner and amount: How and how much should we coercively rehabilitate? I will briefly discuss each of these questions before explaining their applicability to the justification of the specific practice of rehabilitating juvenile offenders.

The Question of Justification. "Why should we ever restrict a violator's liberty, cause pain, or attempt to change a personality or character as part of an attempt to rehabilitate or cure a violator?" This question has a number of possible replies. I mention only two here. One reply would look to the beneficial "direct effect" of rehabilitation and declare that part of the justification of depriving violators' liberty in order to cure them is to be found in the fact that this makes them happy (or, at least, it relieves their misery). This is part of a general utilitarian justification of rehabilitation. The implication is that the good direct effects of therapy outweigh the bad, that is, that although such therapeutic processes as restricting liberty, causing pain, and changing someone's personality are evils, they are ultimately justifiable because they prevent or relieve the greater evil of the person's suffering. Moreover, the utilitarian would contend that the side effects of legal rehabilitation are, on balance, good. Since the offender will not be returned to society until he or she is rehabilitated, society is protected from a repetition of the offense that prompted the initial intervention.

A second possible answer to question (*a*) parallels one form of the retributivist theory of punishment. This answer consists in the claim that no one should be rehabilitated unless he has committed an offense *and* his offense is a symptom of an underlying disease or illness. These are necessary conditions of rehabilitation; criminals should be rehabilitated only if they need or require to be cured. It should be noticed, however, that, unlike the case with retributivist theories of punishment, here there is no notion of *desert*; that is, one does not argue that the "sick" criminal deserves to be rehabilitated, for, unlike punishment, rehabilitation is not a social response intended to make the criminal suffer for what he has done. And yet one might argue that anyone who is sick or ill has a moral claim on society (a claim right) to be cured, in which case there is a reciprocal duty to rehabilitate him ("a sick criminal should not go unrehabilitated"). Indeed, one might argue that there is such a duty whether or not crime is, in fact, reduced by the practice of rehabilitating "sick" criminals. However, in the absence of proof that there is such a claim right, a more plausible variant of this parallel to retributivism would be merely to rule out the permissibility of rehabilitating those who do not need it, and this is recommended on grounds of justice. It is unfair to single out someone and subject him to rehabilitation unless his crime was indeed a manifestation or symptom of an underlying illness. As I will show below, this is in fact the guiding consideration when questions about the appropriate *distribution* of rehabilitation arise.

The Question of Distribution. "Whom should we coercively rehabilitate?" This is the most difficult of the three questions to answer, although the answer is initially derived from the concept of rehabilitation: "Only the sick (those who are suffering) are (by definition) candidates for rehabilitation." What this answer disguises is the root question of why we attach moral importance to restricting therapy to offenders who are "sick" or "suffering." Answers to this question are provided by both the principle of utility and the principle of justice.

However, it might be argued that the principle of utility could be used to justify rehabilitative practices that most of us would regard as morally wrong. For example, utilitarian considerations might conceivably justify subjecting a person who is not believed to be sick or otherwise in need of treatment to a program of rehabilitative therapy. This might be done for two reasons. First, we might wish to deter those who would commit a crime and then attempt to escape punishment by pleading that they were suffering from mental disease at the time they committed the crime. If they were made aware that such persons were nonetheless subjected to lengthy losses of liberty and perhaps to painful programs of treatment, they might be deterred entirely from such conduct. Second, since treatment might involve making a change in someone's personality, it might be thought conducive to the greatest good that we subject a particularly "troublesome" person to such treatment even though he does not otherwise display symptoms of illness or disease. If the "cure" is successful we thereby prevent his repeating his offense in the future and thus maximize the good of all.

In order to avoid these embarrassing cases it is necessary to introduce a principle of justice that requires that the state *restrict* rehabilitation to all and only those whose offending conduct is symptomatic of an underlying illness or disease. Although there may be beneficial consequences that would accrue in a system that occasionally "treated" a person who was not believed to be sick, this is seen to be unjust because the person does not suffer from a condition that makes him relevantly different from others. That is, he has no *need* for treatment; hence, justice requires that he not be subjected to this sort of (coercive) social response to his deviant conduct.

These considerations show why we should *exclude* from rehabilitative treatment at least the following classes of people. First, and most importantly, we must exclude those who "could have done otherwise" than they did when they committed the offense or who "could have avoided it." If either of these things is true for some hypothetical person X, then we cannot also say that X's act was a manifestation or symptom of some inner condition or disease that caused him to act as he did. Hence, there is nothing about what he did that evidences a need for treatment.

Second, we should exclude from programs of rehabilitation those who could not have avoided what they did but whose conduct was caused not by some internal condition from which they were suffering but from something external to them. There will, of course, be difficulty in maintaining a rigid distinction between "internal" and "external" causal conditions, but consider the following examples of the latter: (1) X steals from Y because Z has ordered X to do this and Z has backed up his order with a threat to X's life unless X complies; (2) X holds a knife, and Y against X's will seizes his hand and therewith stabs Y;[4] or (3) X, while driving a car, is attacked by a swarm of bees or hit by a stone and the car is put temporarily out of his control, resulting in a collision with a car driven by Y. It is clear from each of these cases that X does not, by his "conduct," display a need for treatment of an underlying condition that caused the conduct and from which he is currently "suffering."

Third, there is a group of cases in which rehabilitation is not a justifiable response but in which we cannot say with any confidence either that the agent "could have" or "could not have" helped or avoided what he did. Somewhat longer "stories" are used to describe the social, environmental, or cultural factors providing the context in which the deviant behavior occurs. For example: (4) X occupies a lower-class position within the society and does not have the same opportunities for achievement enjoyed by others. He is in a disadvantageous position in the competition for economic rewards that define success and insure conformity. X experiences frustration, and this motivates him to use illegitimate means to achieve the valued end.[5] (5) X desires to conform, but the cultural values to which he wants to conform are in conflict with those of the dominant order. Because he wants to conform, X commits acts regarded as "criminal" by the dominant order.[6] The reason that rehabilitation is not a justifiable state response in either case (4) or case (5) is not because it is inefficacious but ultimately because it would be unjust. There is nothing in the behavior of X that displays a need for treatment; no illness or disease is manifested in his conduct.

Questions of Manner and Amount. "How and how much should we rehabilitate?" First, the type or manner of rehabilitation chosen by the therapist ought to be specifically tailored to the disorder from which the patient is suffering. As argued in part 3, if a paternalistic liberty-limiting response is just, it must meet the end need of the person whose liberty is restricted. In this context, I interpret this to mean that when there is good evidence that a specific treatment will ameliorate a particular disorder, that treatment and only that treatment is to be received by the patient.

Second, the amount of rehabilitative treatment to which a person is subjected depends upon his response to the treatment. There is nothing in a system of rehabilitation analogous to the sort of determinate sentence to which one is normally subject in a system of punishment. In the juvenile rehabilitative system, an offender should be detained until the treatment is complete or until it is clear that the treatment is not promoting a cure. But unlike a system of punishment, a therapy response is not geared to the seriousness of the wrongdoing. There is no attempt to proportion the amount of rehabilitation to the crime. "It is perfectly plausible giving someone who kills a pill and treating for a lifetime within an institution one who has broken a dish and manifested accident proneness."[7]

Rehabilitation, Illness, and the Juvenile Offender

Let us return now to the question posed at the outset of this chapter: What is the justification of responding to *all* persons adjudicated as "juvenile delinquents" with programs of rehabilitation or treatment? This much is clear from the preceding discussion. If justice requires that *only* those whose offending behavior is a manifestation of illness ought to be rehabilitated, then the only way to show that rehabilitation is a just response to juvenile delinquency is to show that most offenders suffer from an illness that is the cause of their delinquent behavior.* This implies, in turn, that their delinquent acts were *not* such that: (*a*) they could have avoided committing them, (*b*) they were caused by some "external condition," or (*c*) they can be "explained" by the sorts of stories presented in cases (4) and (5).

What possible evidence could be brought forth to support such an extraordinary claim? This depends in part upon how we interpret the words *illness* or *internal condition* in the claim "All juvenile offenders suffer from an illness or internal condition which is the cause of their delinquent behavior (or of which their delinquent behavior is a symptom or manifestation)." There are three interpretations of these terms that are worthy of at least brief discussion: (1) illness as a moral disorder, (2) illness as a psychological disorder, and (3) illness as a biological disorder. Is it the case, under any or all of these interpretations, that there is evidence that the juvenile delinquent is suffering from an illness that had the delinquent behavior as its symptom or manifestation?

Moral Disorder. The claim that child law offenders suffer from an internal moral disorder that causes their delinquent behavior is a

*One who defends the present system of rehabilitation need not show that *all* persons adjudicated as juvenile delinquents are ill. He need only show this for most. Thus, utility might require an administrative arrangement in which all juveniles were included under the same sort of treatment. Although I agree that in such a case utility might dictate slight injustice, the arguments below show that there is no evidence to prove that even most juvenile offenders are ill.

theory that nicely fits the vision of the early reformers who established the juvenile courts in this country. Their vision was of

> an institution which would provide for the care and treatment of juveniles who were thought to be potentially good, but suffering from a moral disorder which manifested itself in violation of the law. Before a juvenile's character was distorted and twisted beyond repair, the juvenile court was to initiate a program of moral education to transform the juvenile into a decent, law-abiding citizen. In this way the needs and interest of the juvenile and of society would be served simultaneously.[8]

There is, of course, a sense in which many children, both delinquent and nondelinquent, suffer from moral disorder. That occurs when they are at an early stage of moral development—for example, they base their distinctions between right and wrong on satisfaction of their own needs or on what behavior gets the social approval of their peers or of adults.* But if this is what is meant, then the fact that a delinquent child suffers from moral disorder does not explain his or her delinquency. For example, since both the delinquent and the nondelinquent child who are in the first stage of moral development make moral distinctions based on need satisfaction, the cause of the social deviancy of the former child must be a combination of unsatisfied needs and lack of close parental supervision. That is, the delinquent child becomes delinquent because, desiring to satisfy his unmet needs and lacking parental (or other adult) supervision, he will commit socially deviant acts in order to satisfy his needs. The nondelinquent child either has his needs met or his parents effectively prevent him from commiting socially deviant acts in the attempt to satisfy those needs.

It follows that "moral disorder" must refer to something other than being in an early stage of moral development if we are to find support for the claim that the juvenile delinquent suffers from a moral disorder that is the cause of the delinquency. One such interpretation is that persons suffering from moral disorder have moral beliefs that are erroneous (in that they are in disagreement with the moral norms that are stated in the criminal law) and they cannot help having these beliefs (because, say, they are members of delinquent subcultures). Now it is at least an empirically testable claim that most juvenile delinquents committed deviant acts because they unavoidably had erroneous moral beliefs. Although there is some support for the claim that juvenile delinquents who are members of delinquent subcultures

*See my discussion in chapter 5 of a child's capacity for reasonable choice where a moral standard of reasonableness is used.

have some erroneous moral beliefs,[9] it is reasonable to predict that the evidence would not support the claim for the entire class of juvenile delinquents (including those who are *not* members of delinquent subcultures). It is probably the case that many children who violate the law have moral beliefs that generally conform with those underlying the criminal code.

I suspect, however, that the term *moral disorder* usually refers to no more than a tendency to violate the law, and the sole evidence that juvenile delinquents have such tendencies is that they have (by definition) violated the law. If this is so, then the claim that juvenile delinquents suffer from a moral disorder that has delinquent behavior as its symptom is the tautological claim that juvenile delinquents have committed delinquent acts. As such, the theory of moral disorder is no longer worthy of our attention.

Psychological Disorder. Are the delinquent acts of juveniles the product of a psychological disorder or mental illness from which they are suffering? Allen has argued that juvenile delinquents "are adolescents who are not mentally ill in any sense of the term that meaningfully distinguishes this group of young persons from the population as a whole."[10] Although he does not present empirical evidence for this claim, I suspect that the evidence would show that *many* juvenile delinquents are not mentally ill. In any event, the burden of proof is on those who would assert the contrary. What they must show is that those who commit delinquent acts would fall into one of the accepted diagnostic categories used by psychiatrists in diagnosing mental illness, for example, schizophrenia (of which there are ten different types), manic-depressive illnesses, paranoid states, one of the several neuroses (anxiety, hysterical neuroses, phobias, obsessions, etc.), or one of the personality disorders (paranoia, schizoid personality, etc.). It is interesting to note in this regard that in each case what the diagnostic category provides is a *behavior* pattern, that is, the specific mental illness is defined in terms of behavior typically engaged in by the person who is said to suffer from the disorder. In many cases there is little understanding of the actual cause of the behavior. Hence, if we are to attribute mental illness to all those children who commit delinquent acts, what we must be prepared to show is that such persons *also* display behavior that falls into one of the preceding diagnostic categories. To repeat: there is as yet no evidence that this is true.

Another way to argue that juvenile delinquents suffer from psychological disorder would be from the standpoint of psychoanalytic theory. I shall not repeat the various versions of this theory here. Suppose, however, that one holds to the classical (Freudian) version under which criminality or delinquency is viewed as "an adaptation to tension states" within the individual. That is, while everyone has an internalized control system (ego or superego)* by which he or she resolves internal conflicts (between the ego and the id as well as between the ego and the superego), actual criminal behavior is a manifestation of a weakness in the control system.

One of the main difficulties with any such theory is proof. What evidence can be given for the claim that juvenile delinquency results from weaknesses in the child's internalized control system? Surely the evidence cannot be that he *has* committed an act of juvenile delinquency, for that would make the psychoanalytic claim about the cause of his juvenile delinquency vacuous. Unless such independent evidence is forthcoming, the theory must suffer the same fate as the theory of moral disorder: it is empirically empty.†

However, the most damaging argument against the theory is that it is susceptible to interpretations that argue that deviant behavior is *not* the product of psychological disorder, but that it is often a *normal* adaptation to what is perceived by the juvenile to be an oppressive situation. Thus, Seymour Halleck argues that "there are times when one feels so oppressed that one feels helpless to do anything about it. When this occurs, criminality is one possible adaptation to the feelings of helplessness."[11] Halleck goes on to claim that deviant behavior is actually advantageous; for example, it "offers the possibility of excitement and the opportunity to creatively use abilities and skills normally not ordinarily utilized." The deviant act also "allows the opportunity to locate the source of oppression outside the self and decrease the blame of self," and it "provides a rationale for inade-

*The *ego* is the reality-testing aspect of one's mental life. It "evaluates a situation and logically derives the line of behavior which will maximize pleasure and minimize pain." The *superego* "is roughly equivalent to the idea of conscience in that it attempts to suppress drives and allows feelings of pride when one has lived up to goals and expectations." The *id* signifies "the states of tension created by the sexual and aggressive drives which strive toward satisfaction" (National Institute for Juvenile Justice and Delinquency Prevention, *Working Papers of the National Task Force to Develop Standards and Goals for Juvenile Justice and Delinquency Prevention*, vol. 1, *Preventing Delinquency: A Comparative Analysis of Delinquency Prevention Theory*; 9 vols. [Washington, D.C.: U.S. Department of Justice, 1977], pp. 85–86; Sigmund Freud, *A General Introduction to Psychoanalysis*, trans. Joan Riviere [New York: Washington Square Press, 1962].)

†A large range of facts must be relevant to the psychoanalytic hypothesis, and the hypothesis must be judged on the weight of the total evidence. For the view that it is in principle possible to state the kind of evidence that would count as positive and that which would count as negative, see Wesley C. Salmon, "Psychoanalytic Theory and Evidence," in *Freud: A Collection of Critical Essays*, ed. Richard Wollheim (Garden City, N.Y.: Anchor, 1974), pp. 271–84. However, Salmon does not argue that the hypothesis is empirically confirmed.

quacy." This is a far cry from the behavior of the mentally ill person who instead turns inward in an attempt to alter his or her internal environment by displaying, for instance, depression, a phobia, or an obsession. The criminal, according to some psychoanalysts, is often making a healthy direct attempt to alleviate a feeling of oppression.

Biological Disorder. Biological theories of criminality claim that there is a causal relationship between certain sorts of biological abnormalities and juvenile delinquency. For example, it has been held that there is a relationship between certain chromosomal abnormalities and antisocial, aggressive, or other behaviors likely to be labeled criminal. Again, there are theories claiming that many delinquents suffer from minimal brain dysfunction, especially as this relates to neurological abnormalities, hyperkinesis, reading disorders, and related behavioral characteristics. There are also theories pointing to endocrine abnormalities, especially those where levels of testosterone (the "male" hormone) or progesterone and estrogen (the "female" hormones) appear to be correlated with behavior.

However, to repeat the conclusion recently reached in a wide-ranging study conducted for the National Institute for Juvenile Justice and Delinquency Prevention, "most of the biologically-oriented research . . . is methodologically poor," and there seems to be no general agreement or concordance of findings in the various subject areas discussed:

> Generalizations are made from a handful of cases: typically between two to 20 individuals; no attempt is ever made to develop an adequate sampling plan, let alone carry one out; research designs, where they exist, are inadequate for the kinds of generalizations presented; statistical analyses with hypothesis testing is rarely undertaken; physiological measurements and generalizations are offered without any regard given to the crucially important prerequisites of demonstrated validity and reliability.[12]

In sum, the evidence that delinquent behavior can be traced to biological disorder is both inconclusive and based on "shaky methodological designs."

Conclusions and Recommendations

There is, then, no support for the claim that most children adjudicated as juvenile delinquents suffer from an illness or pathological condition that is the cause of their behavior, when this claim is regarded under the preceding three interpretations of the concept of "illness." Hence, it cannot be justifiable *on grounds of justice* to cause the entire class of juvenile delinquents to be liable to the single disposition of rehabilitation or therapy. Since it is not the case that most delinquents are "ill," they do not display a need for rehabilitation. Hence, the state fails to treat children equally by subjecting them to a mode of social response to their deviant behavior different from that accorded adult violators of the law.

We should note that this is *not* to argue the point that rehabilitation is inefficacious because, for example, by treating juvenile delinquents the system has failed to combat recidivism. For even if the therapeutic response worked, my claim is that it would still be morally wrong (because unjust) to submit all juvenile offenders to therapy.

What, then, would a just system of social response to juvenile delinquency be like? What features must it possess to satisfy the demands of justice? Although I cannot provide here a detailed answer to this question, I should like to conclude this chapter with at least a sketch of what I take to be its central features.

First, once we give up the assumption that most juvenile offenders are ill, we must construct a system of response to juvenile deviancy that allows for a *diversity* of explanations of deviant behavior—explanations that range from "He could have avoided what he did" to "He did it because he was raised in a 'bad neighborhood,' " and "He did it because he suffers from a personality disorder."

Second, if we abandon the idea that the sole aim of the juvenile court should be to rehabilitate the child, we are thrown back on the other important aim of the court, an aim that is often forgotten: to protect the community's interest in its security and well-being. Now in order to accomplish this in a world where we are also to allow for diverse explanation of criminal behavior, it is reasonable to turn to the sort of social response that is characteristic of criminal law: depriving the offender of liberty. This is reasonable because it has the beneficial effect of at least temporarily incapacitating those juveniles found to constitute a threat to the security of others. However, this gives rise to two further questions that must be answered if we are also to fashion a *just* system of social response to juvenile deviancy: (*a*) When (that is, under what conditions) is the state justified in depriving a juvenile of liberty? and (*b*) What further modes of response should the state make to those juveniles who have been deprived of liberty?

Adjudication: The "Clutch Line" for Juvenile Offenders.[13] The juvenile court adjudication hearing can be conceived of as a hearing to establish whether the state has the right to get the juvenile who is before the court into its "clutches," or to deprive him of his liberty. If adjudicated a delinquent, then the juvenile is properly under the state's control. He can no longer decide his own fate, and it is up to the authorities to decide what kind of treatment to impose upon him. Hence, question (*a*) posed above can be restated as the question When does the state have the right to get the juvenile into its clutches, that is, when does he cross the 'clutch line'?

If we can no longer assume that all children who violate the law are ill, then there is no justification for the current practice of permitting a juvenile to fall into the state's clutches on a mere finding that he or she did something prohibited by the criminal law. The moral wrongness in drawing the clutch line at this point is simply that it would allow the state to deprive a juvenile of liberty even when he or she had no fair opportunity to obey the law. And this is precisely the point that we would argue if the state attempted to draw a similar "clutch line" for adult offenders.

It follows that we must at least require for conviction both a prohibited act (*actus reus*) and most of the "mental conditions" included under the terms *mens rea*, for example, knowingly, purposely, negligently, recklessly. Thus, the court should allow as defenses such conditions as reasonable mistake, accident, and loss of muscular or bodily control, that is, defenses that establish that on a particular occasion the child before the court lacked the capacity to conform his conduct to the law. Another defense that the court should allow is one that precludes an entire class of children from being "clutched" by the state, namely, those who are too young to have the requisite mental element. The early common law set the age of this class of children at seven years, but further empirical research should be done to establish precisely at what age we can say with assurance that children below that age do not have the required mental state.

The problem, however, is to decide what *other* mental conditions and their corresponding defenses should be allowed as part of the *mens rea* requirement. In particular, should a child's mental health be a part of the requirement and should mental illness be an affirmative defense? Should a child who is a product of an adverse social environment, corrupting peer influences, etc., have a defense?

I am inclined to answer both questions in the negative. Although prima facie we ought not morally to condemn or blame those who could not have avoided what they did, we do not necessarily hold a juvenile blameworthy in the mere act of allowing him to be clutched by the state. Second, there are important state interests that must be brought into the balance. Thus, the state interest in protecting itself from socially dangerous persons outweighs the interest of such children in being given their freedom at this stage. Third, I have serious doubts that the adjudicatory hearing is an appropriate forum either for determining that a child is mentally ill or for demonstrating that he is a helpless product of a bad social environment. These are matters that are best left to the dispositional stage of the process, where "expert" testimony and more flexible procedural rules will give them full consideration.

Finally, the adjudication hearing should be governed by the procedural rules that characterize proceedings in the adult criminal court. As the Supreme Court recognized in *Gault*, defending a child through adversary proceedings is an especially important matter before the clutch line is crossed, and the sole issue being decided is whether the child is to lose his or her liberty.

Dispositions: What to Do with the Juvenile Delinquent. The real problem for any proposal to change the juvenile court comes after the adjudication hearing in which a decision has been made to keep the juvenile in the clutches of the state. The problem is to match the mode of state response to the individual child who has been adjudicated "delinquent" under the criteria set forth above. At present there is only one mode of social response to juvenile delinquency: rehabilitation. However, if it is true that there are diverse explanations of juvenile deviancy, then there must also be diverse modes of response to the delinquent child. Indeed, as I have argued above, it is not only unreasonable but it is unjust to refuse to match the mode of state response to the individual child.

There should be a variety of responses available to the juvenile court, ranging from punishment to outright release. In between these extremes the court should have the capability of granting such dispositions as parole under supervision, assignment to a mental hospital, rehabilitative work camps, or placement in "places of safety."

Second, in order to tailor the type of response to the individual child, the court should appoint panels of "experts," for example, child psychologists, sociologists, or moralists, to conduct psychosocial studies of and interviews with the delinquent child, bringing to bear all possible data that might account for the delinquent behavior. The panel would present its evidence and make recommendations to a post–clutch-line judge or committee of judges. The child's lawyer should be present to challenge the findings of the panel if he wishes, but the dispositional hearing need not be bound by all of the procedural rules of the adjudication hearing.

There are a variety of possible responses that the committee might decide to make to the juvenile before it. First, one can easily imagine circumstances in which it might be both just and reasonable to punish children, especially older children. Suppose that a sixteen-year-old child decided to commit a crime knowing that he risked losing his liberty if he should be caught. Suppose further that he is caught and adjudicated a delinquent. At the dispositional stage, the panel of experts can find no evidence that he is suffering from a mental illness or that he is the product of an adverse environment. In a case such as this it might be that punishment (understood as society's harsh expression of blame) is the only just and reasonable disposition. Punishment may be reasonable because it may have the *extra*punitive effect of deterring the child from repeating the offense. It is a (retributively) just response because society "exacts the debt" owed to it by the voluntary offender who has taken something from it and must now give it back.

In other cases the proper disposition might be assignment to a mental hospital or a rehabilitative work camp, depending on the type of illness from which the juvenile is found to suffer. In order to guard against the child's falling permanently under the arbitrary power of some doctor or administrator who regards him as too dangerous (ill) ever to be released, we must keep as much protection of due process at every stage as is possible. The condition of every child in a rehabilitative unit must be actively investigated by an autonomous agency at regular intervals, and the agency should be available continuously to receive complaints. Moreover, there should be elaborate procedures for appeals of decisions of both the therapeutic authorities and autonomous agencies.

The most difficult cases for the committee of judges to decide will undoubtedly be those in which the child's delinquency is found to be a product of his social setting. Here I am inclined to agree with the contention of Professors Allen,[14] Schur,[15] and Hazard[16] that the juvenile court lacks and probably will never be given the legal authority and administrative competence to intervene on the scale required by the alleged cause of the delinquency. What is called for is reform of the social and economic structure in which the delinquent youth finds himself, and this in turn entails that the court institute broad programs of social justice directed toward the socioeconomic classes and ethnic groups among which criminal conduct is highly evidenced. Moreover, the court lacks and probably will never have the political and fiscal resources necessary to commission other institutions to intervene.

In such cases it may be that the most that the juvenile court will be able to do is to deprive the juvenile delinquent of liberty for a fixed period of time without making any judgment of blame, thereby at least satisfying the interest of the community in being free from harm (if even for only a short period). At the same time the court will have come as close as it can to providing the blameless delinquent what he needs: a change of environment. There is, of course, nothing to prevent the court from doing what it can to aid the youth in eventually escaping his poor environment. It could, for example, initiate voluntary vocational training programs for incarcerated youths, at the same time encouraging labor unions to admit, and skilled craftsmen to accept as apprentices, juvenile delinquents upon release. Although such programs do little to break down the deleterious influence of the youth's immediate social environment (family, peers, neighborhood), they may cause him to notice the unfavorable comparisons between it and other environments and thus encourage him to make an eventual escape.

In sum, I do not claim that my (general) proposals for reform of the juvenile court will substantially reduce juvenile crime. My purpose was not to recommend a system of social response to combat recidivism, although I believe that this is an important consideration when social utility is the relevant moral principle. Rather, my aim was to sketch the characteristics of a *just* institution of social response to juvenile crime and, secondly, to show that the present rehabilitative system does not meet the demands of the principle of justice. Although this principle may not always lead us to recommend what is required by utility, if we are to achieve a juvenile court that can stand as a paradigm of a morally correct social institution, then justice must be a principle given as much weight as utility in the construction of the material adjudicatory and dispositional rules of the court.*

*After writing this chapter, I came across Martin Guggenheim's call to abolish the juvenile justice system and eliminate jurisdiction over status offenders. His central point, as is mine, is that the state does an injustice to children by proclaiming that the jurisdiction of the juvenile court is primarily to help them. We differ only in that, whereas I would retain a separate court system to deal with young criminal offenders, he proposes integration with the adult court system ("A Call to Abolish the Juvenile Justice System," *Children's Rights Report*, vol. 2, no. 9 [June 1978]: 3–11).

Notes

Chapter 1

1. Paul Adams, et al., *Children's Rights* (New York: Praeger, 1971), p. 1.
2. *Planned Parenthood of Central Missouri* v. *Danforth,* 428 U.S. 52 (1976).
3. H. C. Black, *Black's Law Dictionary,* 4th ed. rev. (St. Paul, Minn.: West Publishing Co., 1968).
4. Joel Feinberg, *Social Philosophy* (Englewood Cliffs, N.J.: Prentice-Hall, 1973), p. 2.
5. Ibid., p. 3.
6. Ibid.
7. I owe this approach to the problem of defining rights to Lawrence Becker, *Property Rights: Philosophic Foundations* (Boston: Routledge and Kegan Paul, 1977), chap. 2.
8. Wesley Newcomb Hohfeld, *Fundamental Legal Conceptions* (New Haven: Yale University Press, 1919).
9. Becker, *Property Rights,* p. 11.
10. Feinberg, *Social Philosophy*, pp. 59–60.
11. Becker, *Property Rights,* p. 12.
12. Ibid.
13. Ibid., p. 13.
14. Hohfeld, *Fundamental Legal Conceptions*, p. 60.
15. Ibid., p. 15.
16. Feinberg, *Social Philosophy*, p. 85.
17. "The Model of Rules," 35 U. Chi. L. Rev. (1967).
18. Ibid., p. 22.
19. A. Gewirth, ed., *Political Philosophy* (London: Macmillan, 1965), p. 5.
20. *Utilitarianism* (New York: Bobbs-Merrill, 1957), p. 66 (chap. 5, para. 25).
21. See, for example, Richard Farson, *Birthrights: A Bill of Rights for Children* (New York: Macmillan Co., 1974), p. 9.

Chapter 2

1. See especially Alan Sussman, *The Rights of Young People: The Basic A.C.L.U. Guide to a Young Person's Rights* (New York: Avon, 1977). Other more dated treatises with fewer annotations include: Irving Sloan, *Youth and the Law*, 2nd ed. (New York: Oceana, 1974), and Michael Dorman, *Under 21: A Young People's Guide to Legal Rights* (New York: Delacorte, 1971).
2. Monrad G. Paulsen and Charles H. Whitebread, *Juvenile Law and Procedure* (Reno, Nev.: National Council of Juvenile Court Judges, 1974), p. 1.
3. Bernard Flexner and Reuben Oppenheimer, *The Legal Aspect of the Juvenile Court*, Children's Bureau Publication no. 99 (1922), p. 9, reprinted (in part) in Orman W. Ketchem and Monrad G. Paulsen, *Juvenile Courts: Cases and Materials* (Brooklyn: The Foundation Press, 1967), pp. 4–5.

4. Paulsen and Whitebread, *Juvenile Law*, p. 60.
5. Alfred Kadushin, "Child Welfare Services," *Children Today* 5 (1976): 21–22.
6. National Institute for Juvenile Justice and Delinquency Prevention, *Working Papers of the National Task Force to Develop Standards and Goals for Juvenile Justice and Delinquency Prevention,* vol. 6, *Abuse and Neglect: A Comparative Analysis of Standards and State Practices*; 9 vols. (Washington, D.C.: U.S. Department of Justice, 1977), p. 56.
7. A. J. Kleinfeld, "The Balance of Power among Infants, Their Parents and the State, Part 2," *Family Law Quarterly* 5 (1972): 431.
8. Sussman, *Rights of Young People*, p. 151.
9. Michael S. Wald, "State Intervention on Behalf of 'Neglected' Children: A Search for Realistic Standards," in *Pursuing Justice for the Child*, ed. Margaret Rosenheim (Chicago: University of Chicago Press, 1976), pp. 265–66.
10. See George E. Stevens, "The Reputation Rights of Infants," *Family Law Quarterly* 5 (1972): 435–36, for a discussion and citation of cases.
11. *Merriken* v. *Cressman*, 364 F. Supp. 913 (1973).
12. *People* v. *Overton*, 20 N.Y. 2d 360, 229 N.E.2d 596, 283 N.Y.S.2d 222 (1967). The court asserted that school officials possess not only the right but the affirmative duty to search school lockers and desks when they suspect that they contain illegal items.
13. Kleinfeld, "Balance of Power," p. 413.
14. *Pierce* v. *Society of Sisters*, 268 U.S. 510 (1925).
15. *Wisconsin* v. *Yoder*, 406 U.S. 205 (1972).
16. *Guzick* v. *Drebus*, 431 F.2d 594 (6th Cir. 1970), *cert. denied* 401 U.S. 948 (1971).
17. *Hughes* v. *Caddo Parish School Board*, 57 F. Supp. 508 (W. D. La. 1944) *aff'd* 323 U.S. 685 (1945).
18. *Tinker* v. *Des Moines Independent School District*, 393 U.S. 503 (1969).
19. *West Virginia State Board of Education* v. *Barnette*, 319 U.S. 624 (1943).
20. Goldstein, "Child Labor," p. 34.
21. *Bykofsky* v. *Borough of Middletown*, 401 F. Supp. 1242 (M.D. Pa. 1975).
22. See Sussman, *Rights of Young People*, chap. 11, for a complete account of state laws in this area.
23. Walter Wadlington, "Minors and Health Care: The Age of Consent," *Osgoode Hall L. J.* 73 (1973): 121.
24. *Planned Parenthood of Central Missouri* v. *Danforth*, 428 U.S. 52 (1976).
25. *Carey* v. *Population Services International*, 431 U.S. 678 (1977).
26. John D. Calamari and J. M. Perillo, *The Law of Contracts* (St. Paul, Minn.: West Publishing Co., 1970), p. 201.
27. *In re Gault*, 387 U.S. 1 (1967).
28. *In re Winship*, 397 U.S. 358 (1970).
29. *McKeiver* v. *Pennsylvania*, 403 U.S. 528 (1971).
30. Ibid., at 543.
31. *Goss* v. *Lopez*, 419 U.S. 565 (1975).
32. William L. Prosser, *Law of Torts,* 4th ed. (St. Paul, Minn.: West Publishing Co., 1971): p. 997.
33. Ibid.
34. Vincent DeFrancis, "Termination of Parental Rights: Balancing the Equities," in *Legal Rights of Children* (New York: Practicing Law Institute, 1973), p. 105.
35. Paulsen and Whitebread, *Juvenile Law*, p. 55.
36. Ibid., p. 57.
37. National Institute for Juvenile Justice and Delinquency Prevention, *Abuse and Neglect*, p. 36.

Chapter 3

1. 393 U.S. 503 (1969).
2. Ibid., at 509.
3. 390 U.S. 629 (1968).
4. 321 U.S. 158 (1944), at 168.

5. 390 U.S. 629 (1968), at 650.
6. 428 U.S. 52 (1976).
7. Ibid., at 75.
8. 431 U.S. 678 (1977).
9. 428 U.S. 52 (1976), at 95.
10. Ibid., at 102.
11. Joel Feinberg, *Social Philosophy* (Englewood Cliffs, N.J.: Prentice-Hall, 1973), p. 81.
12. 387 U.S. 1 (1967).
13. Ibid., at 27–28.
14. Ibid., at 79–80.
15. *Kent* v. *United States*, 383 U.S. 541 (1966), at 556.
16. 387 U.S. 1 (1967), at 22.
17. Feinberg, *Social Philosophy*.

Chapter 4

1. H. C. Black, *Black's Law Dictionary*, 4th ed. rev. (St. Paul, Minn.: West Publishing Co., 1968), p. 906.
2. See chapter 2.
3. For an interesting discussion of Locke's views on parental ownership of children, see Robert Nozick, *Anarchy, State and Utopia* (New York: Basic Books, 1974), pp. 287–89, and Lawrence C. Becker, *Property Rights: Philosophic Foundations* (Boston: Routledge and Kegan Paul, 1977), pp. 36–41.
4. Immanuel Kant, *Foundations of the Metaphysics of Morals*, trans. Lewis White Beck (New York: Liberal Arts Press, 1959).
5. John Locke, *An Essay concerning the True Original, Extent and End of Civil Government* (London: Awnsham Churchill, 1690).
6. R. S. Downie and Elizabeth Telfer, *Respect for Persons* (London: George Allen and Unwin, 1969), pp. 20–21.
7. Locke, *Essay*, chap. 2.
8. Kant, *Foundations*, p. 39.
9. James W. Cornman and Keith Lehrer, *Philosophical Problems and Arguments: An Introduction* (New York: Macmillan Co., 1968), p. 421.
10. *Kant: The Philosophy of Right* (London: Macmillan & Co., 1970), p. 52.
11. "The Child in the Moral Order," *Philosophy* 52 (April 1977): 171.
12. Lawrence Kohlberg, "Moral Development and the Education of Adolescents," in *Adolescents and the American High School*, ed. R. F. Purnell (New York: Holt, Rinehart and Winston, 1970); idem, "Development of Moral Character and Moral Ideology," in M. L. Hoffman and L. W. Hoffman, eds., *Review of Child Development Research* (New York: Russell Sage Foundation, 1964).
13. Kohlberg, "Moral Character," p. 154.
14. Cf. Cornman and Lehrer, *Philosophical Problems*, p. 422.
15. *Social Statics* (London: William & Norgate, 1868), p. 194.
16. James Rachels, "Do Animals Have a Right to Liberty?," in Tom Regan and Peter Singer, eds., *Animal Rights and Human Obligations* (Englewood Cliffs, N.J.: Prentice-Hall, 1976), p. 214.
17. E.g., by Downie and Telfer, *Respect for Persons*, p. 59.
18. Ibid.
19. Jonathan Glover, *Causing Death and Saving Lives* (London: Penguin, 1977), p. 70.

Chapter 5

1. This is John Stuart Mill's definition of a right. See *Utilitarianism* (New York: Bobbs-Merrill, 1957), p. 66.
2. William Frankena, *Ethics*, 2nd ed. (Englewood Cliffs, N.J.: Prentice-Hall, 1973), p. 45.

3. Cf. J. Kemp, *Reason, Action and Morality* (New York: Humanities Press, 1964), p. 101.

4. Stephen Toulmin, "The Concept of Stages in Psychological Development," in *Cognitive Development and Epistemology*, ed. T. Mischel (New York: Academic Press, 1971), pp. 25–71.

5. National Center for Health Statistics, *Facts of Life and Death* (Washington, D.C.: U.S. Department of Health, Education, and Welfare, 1976), p. 33. It should also be noted that the category of "accidental deaths" includes motor vehicle accidents as well as accidental deaths caused by falls, poisoning by solid and liquid substances, etc. One could hardly maintain that deaths of children caused in motor vehicle accidents provide evidence that children are accident prone!

6. Herbert Ginzberg and Sylvia Opper, *Piaget's Theory of Intellectual Development: An Introduction* (Englewood Cliffs, N.J.: Prentice-Hall, 1969), p. 181.

7. W. E. Martin and C. B. Stendler, *Child Behavior and Development* (New York: Harcourt, Brace and World, 1959), p. 559.

Chapter 6

1. Joel Feinberg, *Social Philosophy* (Englewood Cliffs, N.J.: Prentice-Hall, 1973), p. 21.

2. John Stuart Mill, *On Liberty* (New York: Liberal Arts Press, 1956), p. 71.

3. Ibid., p. 14.

4. Francis Schrag, "The Child in the Moral Order," *Philosophy* 52 (April 1977): 175.

5. Francis Schrag, "Rights over Children," *Journal of Value Inquiry* 7 (1973): 101–2.

6. Ibid., p. 104.

7. R. S. Downie and Elizabeth Telfer, *Respect for Persons* (London: George Allen and Unwin, 1969), p. 83.

8. John Stuart Mill, *Utilitarianism* (New York: Bobbs-Merrill, 1957), p. 58.

9. William Frankena, *Ethics,* 2nd ed. (Englewood Cliffs, N.J.: Prentice-Hall, 1973), p. 42.

Chapter 7

1. I owe this point to Jeffrie G. Murphy. See his article "Rights and Borderline Cases," *Arizona Law Review* 19, no. 1 (1978): 232 and 235.

2. John Rawls, *A Theory of Justice* (Cambridge, Mass.: Harvard University Press, 1971).

3. Ibid., p. 250.

4. Ibid., pp. 248–49.

5. Ibid., p. 249.

6. Ibid.

7. Ibid.

8. Ibid., pp. 249–50.

9. Ibid., p. 250.

10. John D. Hodson, "The Principle of Paternalism," *American Philosophical Quarterly* 14 (January 1977): 67.

11. Ronald Dworkin, "Paternalism," in *Morality and the Law,* ed. R. Wasserstrom (Belmont, Calif.: Wadsworth, 1971), p. 121.

12. See Norman Daniels, ed., *Reading Rawls: Critical Studies on Rawls' A Theory of Justice* (New York: Basic Books, 1976).

13. Thomas Nagel, "Rawls on Justice," in ibid., p. 8.

14. Ibid.

Chapter 8

1. Jonathon Glover, *Causing Death and Saving Lives* (London: Penguin, 1977), p. 79.

2. Cf. Joel Feinberg, *Social Philosophy* (Englewood Cliffs, N.J.: Prentice-Hall, 1973), p. 100; William K. Frankena, "Some Beliefs about Justice," in *Philosophy of Law*, ed. Joel

Feinberg and Hyman Gross (Belmont, Calif.: Dickenson, 1975), pp. 250–51.

3. Feinberg, *Social Philosophy*, p. 104.

4. H. L. A. Hart, *The Concept of Law* (Oxford: Oxford University Press, 1961), p. 159.

5. Frankena, "Justice," p. 257.

6. Ibid., pp. 255–56.

Chapter 9

1. John Rawls, *A Theory of Justice* (Cambridge, Mass.: Harvard University Press, 1971), p. 62.

2. Joel Feinberg, *Social Philosophy* (Englewood Cliffs, N.J.: Prentice-Hall, 1973), p. 26.

3. Cf. Joel Feinberg's remarks on the considerations that complicate the delicate task of interest balancing in "Limits to the Free Expression of Opinion," in *Philosophy of Law*, ed. Joel Feinberg and Hyman Gross (Belmont, Calif.: Dickenson, 1975), pp. 141–42.

4. Joseph Goldstein, Anna Freud, and Albert J. Solnit, *Beyond the Best Interests of the Child* (New York: The Free Press, 1973), p. 54.

5. I owe some of the distinctions in this section to William J. Winslade, "Human Needs and Human Rights," in *Human Rights: Initial Publication of the American Section of the International Association for Philosophy of Law and Social Philosophy, Consisting of Papers Prepared for Its Second Plenary Meeting*, ed. Ervin H. Pollack (Buffalo, N.Y.: Jay Stewart Publication, 1971), pp. 24–37. However, the distinction between "means needs" and "end needs" is mine.

6. Cf. Feinberg, *Social Philosophy*, p. 16.

7. William Frankena, *Ethics*, 2nd ed. (Englewood Cliffs, N.J.: Prentice-Hall, 1973), p. 53.

Chapter 10

1. National Institute for Juvenile Justice and Delinquency Prevention, *Working Papers of the National Task Force to Develop Standards and Goals for Juvenile Justice and Delinquency Prevention*, vol. 5, *Jurisdiction: Status Offenses: A Comparative Analysis of Standards and State Practices;* 9 vols. (Washington, D.C.: U.S. Department of Justice, 1977), p. 10.

2. Ibid., p. 5.

3. Ibid.

Chapter 11

1. National Institute for Juvenile Justice and Delinquency Prevention, *Working Papers of the National Task Force to Develop Standards and Goals for Juvenile Justice and Delinquency Prevention*, vol. 6, *Abuse and Neglect: A Comparative Analysis of Standards and State Practices*; 9 vols. (Washington, D.C.: U.S. Department of Justice, 1977), p. 13.

2. Ibid.

3. Michael S. Wald, "State Intervention on Behalf of 'Neglected' Children: A Search for Realistic Standards," in *Pursuing Justice for the Child*, ed. Margaret Rosenheim (Chicago: University of Chicago Press, 1976), p. 262.

4. Sheldon White, *Federal Programs for Young Children: Review and Recommendations*, vol. 2 (Washington, D.C.: Government Printing Office, 1973): 240.

5. Wald, " 'Neglected' Children," pp. 262–65.

6. Ibid.; White, *Young Children*, 1: p. 74.

7. Joint Commission on Mental Health of Children, *Crisis in Mental Health: Challenge for the 1970's: Report* (New York: Harper and Row, 1970), p. 250.

8. Joseph Goldstein, Anna Freud, and Albert J. Solnit, *Beyond the Best Interests of the Child* (New York: The Free Press, 1973).

9. Ibid., p. 20.

10. Ibid.
11. White, *Young Children*, p. 240.
12. Wald, " 'Neglected' Children," p. 260.
13. Ibid., p. 262.
14. National Research Council, Advisory Committee in Child Development, *Toward a National Policy for Children and Families* (Washington, D.C.: National Academy of Sciences, 1976), p. 5.

Chapter 12

1. Martin P. Golding, *Philosophy of Law* (Englewood Cliffs, N.J.: Prentice-Hall, 1975), p. 70.
2. Herbert Morris, "Persons and Punishment," in *Human Rights*, ed. A. I. Melden (Belmont, Calif.: Wadsworth, 1970), p. 122.
3. The reader will note an analogy between this way of dividing the problem of rehabilitation and the approach adopted in discussing the problem of punishment in H. L. A. Hart, *Punishment and Responsibility* (Oxford: Clarendon Press, 1968), p. 4.
4. This and the next example are from ibid., pp. 95–96.
5. This is the sort of explanation of juvenile misconduct characteristic of "social control" theories of delinquency. See Robert K. Merten, "Social Structure and Anomie," *American Sociological Review* 3 (1937): 672–82.
6. This explanation of juvenile misconduct is typical of the "subcultural" theories of juvenile delinquency. See, for example, Albert K. Cohen, *Delinquent Boys: The Culture of the Gang* (New York: The Free Press, 1955); Marvin E. Wolfgang and Franco Ferracuti, *The Subculture of Violence: Toward an Integrated Theory in Criminology* (London: Tavistock, 1967).
7. Morris, "Persons and Punishment," p. 123.
8. William Winslade, "The Juvenile Courts: From Idealism to Hypocrisy," *Social Theory and Practice* 3 (1974): 183.
9. National Institute for Juvenile Justice and Delinquency Prevention, *Working Papers of the National Task Force to Develop Standards and Goals for Juvenile Justice and Delinquency Prevention*, vol. 1, *Preventing Delinquency: A Comparative Analysis of Delinquency Prevention Theory*; 9 vols. (Washington, D.C.: U.S. Dept. of Justice, 1977), p. 70.
10. Francis A. Allen, *The Borderland of Criminal Justice* (Chicago: University of Chicago Press, 1964), chap. 3.
11. Seymour L. Halleck, *Psychiatry and the Dilemma of Crime* (New York: Harper and Row, 1967), p. 59.
12. National Institute for Juvenile Justice and Delinquency Prevention, *Preventing Delinquency*, p. 127.
13. This and the following section has been inspired by recommendations made by Joel Feinberg for dealing with adult criminals, especially those who are mentally ill. I find some of his ideas extremely well suited to the juvenile court. See his essay, "Crime, Clutchability, and Individuated Treatment," in *Doing and Deserving*, ed. Joel Feinberg (Princeton: Princeton University Press, 1970), pp. 252–71.
14. Allen, *Borderland,* chap. 3.
15. Edwin M. Schur, *Radical Nonintervention: Rethinking the Delinquency Problem* (Englewood Cliffs, N.J.: Prentice-Hall, 1973).
16. Geoffrey C. Hazard, Jr., "The Jurisprudence of Juvenile Deviance," in *Pursuing Justice for the Child*, ed. Margaret Rosenheim (Chicago: University of Chicago Press, 1976), pp. 3–19.

Index

"Actual" moral agency. *See* Moral agency, argument from "actual"

Adjudication hearings, 18; due process rules governing, 28, 39—41; recommendations for, 151. See also *In re Gault*

Adult: competent, 47; definition of, 47; rights of, 48, 49 n, 50

Aid to Families with Dependent Children, 19

A-liberties, legal, 47; arguments for denying to children, 52, 58, 62, 76, 87

Allen, Francis A., 152

Ariès, Philippe, 48 n

Autonomy: moral right to have, respected by others, 96; protected by legal rights, 105

Bad: definition of, 106; list of things regarded as, 106

Becker, Lawrence, 7, 9

Beneficence: argument from, 62—64, 95; objection to argument from, 64—65; principle of, 61, 64—65

Benevolence, character trait of, 106

"Best interests of the child," standard of, 31; used in making child custody decisions, 107—8; used in termination of parental rights proceedings, 31

Biological disorder, theories of, for explaining delinquent behavior, 148

Blackmun, Justice, 78 n

Blackstone, William, 18 n

Carey v. *Population Services International,* 38

Categorical imperative, 51

C-claims, legal, 47; arguments for granting to children, 57—58, 62, 74 n, 85 n

Character, development of, in children, 106

Child, definition of, 47. *See also* Children

Childhood, myth of, 48 n

Child labor: during the industrial revolution, 25 n; justice of present laws regarding, 98; present laws regarding, 25

Child liberationist, 15

Child neglect: debate about laws regarding, 130—31; definition of, 129; present laws regarding, 19—20; recommendations about laws regarding, 134—37

Child protectionist, 15

Child psychology, recent experimental work in, 69

Children: competence of, 3, 32, 68—72; status of, in early Common law, 23 n; status of, in present U.S. law, 17—32; status of, in Roman law, 23 n; studies of moral development in, 54; Supreme Court conception of, as "persons," 42

Children's rights: to autonomy, 57, 97; to be treated as persons, 57 n; to due process, 9, 39—41; to earnings, 20; to education, 19; to liberty, 85, 98; to medical care, 19; to privacy, 21, 37—39; to proper home, 19; to proper moral environment, 19; to rehabilitation, 17, 138—53; to symbolic expression of opinion, 24, 34—37; to undamaged reputation, 21; to vote, 27, 85; to welfare services, 19; to work, 24. *See also* Claims; Immunities, legal; Liberties; Mixed rights

Children's rights movement, dilemma facing, 16

Choice, rational. *See* Rational choice

Claims: capacity, 7; negative, 6—7; positive, 6—7, 17—18, 31. *See also* C-claims, legal

"Clutch-line," concept of, in juvenile court proceedings, 150

Common law: legal power of father over child in, 23 n; status of child in, 23 n

Community interests, 79

Constitutional rights. *See* Rights, constitutional

Contracts: "void," 27; "voidable," 27

"Correct" choice, 66

Criminal courts, trying children in, 41, 152—53

Criminal law, children subject to prohibitions of, 25

Curfew laws, juvenile. *See* Juvenile curfew laws

Defenses, types of, allowed in adjudication hearings, 150—51
Deontological arguments for granting or denying legal rights. *See* Moral agency, argument from "actual"; Moral agency, argument from "potential"
Deontological principles. *See* Normative principles, deontological
Dispositional hearing, 19; recommendations for, 151—52
Distributive justice. *See* Justice, equalitarian principle of
Duties: imperfect, 50; perfect, 50
Dworkin, Ronald M., 11, 12

Emotional harm, as basis for juvenile court jurisdiction, 135
Empirical research, need for, in discussions about children's rights, 72—73
End-needs, 111; "basic," 133; and the good life, 112—14; and neglect statutes, 133—34; standard of "basic," 135—36; and status offenses, 125, 127
Equalitarian justice. *See* Justice, equalitarian principle of
Evil. *See* Bad, definition of
Extrinsic value. *See* Value, extrinsic

Feinberg, Joel, 42 n
First Amendment, rights of children under, 34—37, 42, 43
Fortas, Justice, 34, 40, 41
Fourth Amendment, applicability of, to searches and seizures involving children, 21—22
Frankena, William, 61, 99, 105 n
Freud, Sigmund, 147 n

Ginsberg v. *State of New York,* 5—7
Goldstein, Harold, 23 n, 25 n
Good: definition of, 106; list of things that are, 106
Good life: conception of, in neglect laws, 133; theories of, 113
Goodman, Paul, 3, 15
Guggenheim, Martin, 153 n

Halleck, Seymour, 157
Harm: and definition of an evil, 106; specific, in language of neglect statutes, 130
Hazard, Geoffrey C., 152
Hohfeld, W. N., 6—8, 29

Illness. *See* Biological disorder, theories of, for explaining delinquent behavior; Psychological disorder, theories of, for explaining delinquent behavior
Immunities, legal, of children, 29, 32
Ingraham v. *Wright,* 20 n
Inhelder, B., 71 n
In loco parentis, doctrine of, 22, 23
In re Gault, 39—41, 138, 151
Interest, definition of, in law, 105
Interests: legally recognized, 105—6; and principles of "practicality," 108—10; recognition of, in neglect statutes, 123—24; relative value of, 107—10
Intrinsic value. *See* Value, intrinsic

Jurisprudence, definition of, 4
Justice: equalitarian principle of, 80, 97—100; implications of, for juvenile court, 148—53; implications of, for neglect laws, 132—34; implications of, for status offense legislation, 124–25; moral rights and, 97,103; need as a standard of relevance in, 101; paternalistic legal restrictions required by, 102—3, 114; Rawls's theory of, 80, 84
Juvenile courts: adjudicatory hearings in, 39—40; due process rights in, 28, 40; philosophy of, 16; terminology used in, 18—19
Juvenile curfew laws, 25; evaluation of, using principles of "practicality," 108—10, 111—12
Juvenile delinquency, just system of social response to, 148—53
Juvenile delinquent: definition of, 18—19; high recidivism rate of those adjudicated as, 41
Juvenile status offenses, 25; debate over, 119—21; recommendations on legislation creating, 126—28

Kant, Immanuel, 50
Kantian argument for denying A-liberties to children, 52
Kleinfeld, A. J., 27 n
Kohlberg, Lawrence, 54

Legal principles. *See* Normative principles, legal
Liabilities: legal, of children, 29; to termination of right to be cared for by parent, 29—30; for torts, 29

Liberties, 7—8; of children, at home, 22—23; of children, in school, 23—24; of children, outside of home and school, 24—26; legal, 8; natural, 8
Ling, C. B., 70n
Locke, John, 50, 52

Means-needs, 110—11, 133
Merrill, M. E., 70n
Meyer v. *Nebraska,* 34n
Mill, John Stuart, 14, 75—77, 80
Mixed rights: definition of, 26; to due process, 28; to execute a will, 27; to make contracts, 27; to marry, 26; to sue and recover for torts, 27; to vote, 27
Moral agency: argument from "actual," 52; argument from "potential," 58
Moral agent, definition of, 50
Moral beliefs, erroneous, 145—46
Moral development, early stages of, as evidence of moral disorder in children, 145
Moral disorder, as cause of delinquent behavior, 144—45
Moral principles. *See* Normative principles, moral
Moral rights. *See* Rights, moral
Morris, Herbert, 57n, 140
Murphy, Jeffrey, 51

Nagel, Thomas, 90, 91n
Narveson, Jan, 80n
Natural N-rights. *See* N-rights, natural
Natural rights. *See* Rights, natural
Need: definition of, 110—11; as standard of relevance in principle of equalitarian justice, 101—2. *See also* End-needs; Means-needs
Negative claim rights. *See* Claims, negative
Neglect. *See* Child neglect
Nicholas, Barry, 23n
Normative principles: deontological, 13—14; discovery of, 12—13; legal, 11; moral, 11; nature of, 11—12; of paternalism, 12; questions about, 10—11; teleological, 14
N-rights, natural, 53—56

Original position, idea of, in Rawls's theory, 84

Parens patriae, doctrine of, 6
Parent, definition of, 47. *See also* Parental rights; Parents
Parental authority, child's disregard of, 127
Parental behavior, mention of, in child neglect laws, 131
Parental right: termination of, by state, 29—31; universe of, over children, 22—23
Parents: conception of, of good life for children, 113—14; consent of, to police search of child's room, 21; duties of, to provide care for children, 19—20; freedom of, to choose child's school, 22; as guardian of child's person, 22; interests of, in having liberty of children restricted, 78; physical force used by, in child discipline, 20; status offense laws aiding, in rearing children, 120. *See also* Parental rights
Paterfamilias, concept of, in Roman law, 23
Paternalism: derived from principle of equalitarian justice, 114—16; principle of, 86; in Rawls's theory, 86—87; rough definition of, 3; in Supreme Court decisions, 35—36
Paternalistic restrictions on liberty: direct effects of, 75—78; purpose of laws creating, 98; side effects of, 78—79
Person, definition of, 50
Piaget, J., 71n
Pierce v. *Society of Sisters,* 34n
Planned Parenthood of Central Missouri v. *Danforth,* 37, 42, 78n
Positive claim rights. *See* Claims, positive
"Potential" moral agency. *See* Moral agency, argument from "potential"
Powers, 8
"Practicality," principles of, 108—10
Primary goods, 84
Prince v. *Commonwealth of Massachusetts,* 35
Psychological disorder: interpretation of, in psychoanalytic theory, 146—47; status offenses as symptomatic of, 121—22; theories of, for explaining delinquent behavior, 146—48; types of, 144—48
Punishment: corporal, 20n; definition of, 139; rehabilitation contrasted with, 139

Query, Joy M. N., 71n

Rational choice: children's capacity for, 36, 63, 68—72, 75—76, 87, 89; definition of "lacks the capacity for," 66—68; status offenses and, 125
Rational will. *See* Moral agent, definition of
Rawls, John, 83—85, 105
Rehabilitation: compared to punishment, 138—39; definition of, 138; need for justification of, 139—40; problem of justifying, 140—44; as response to social deviancy, 139

Rehnquist, Justice, 38
Right holders, 6
Right not to be abused, 20—21; and corporal punishment, 20
Right of privacy, 37—39. See also *Carey* v. *Population Services International; Planned Parenthood of Central Missouri* v. *Danforth; Roe* v. *Wade*
Right regarders, 6
Right relationships, 6
Rights: concept of, 5; constitutional, 42; defined by source of justification, 9; human, 10; inalienable, 50; Kantian ethics and, 51; kinds of, 6—9; legal, 9—10; legally protectable, 105; liberty, 22—26, 85; moral, 10; natural, 10, 50; negative list of, 50; normative theory of legal, 4; philosophical problem of children's, 15; positive, 129; students', 24. *See also* Children's rights; Claims; Immunities, legal; Liberties; Mixed rights; Parental rights
Roe v. *Wade,* 39
Roman law, status of child in, 23n

Salmon, Wesley C., 147n
School disciplinary hearings, due process rights of child in, 28
Schrag, Francis, 53, 54, 77, 89
Schur, Edwin M., 152
Self-determining, ability to be. *See* Moral agent, definition of
Self-legislating, ability to be. *See* Moral agent, definition of
Self-legislating beings, 13
Self-realization: and happiness, 77—78; interference with process of, 76—77
Skolnik, Arlene, 69n
Social contract: argument from, 95; theory of, 83
Social philosophy, definition of, 4
Social policy questions remaining after Supreme Court decisions, 42—44
Spencer, Herbert, 56
Status offenses: arguments for abolishing laws that create, 120—21; definition of, 119; justification of laws that create, 119—21
Stevens, Justice, 38, 39
Stewart, Justice, 35, 40, 41
Students' rights. *See* Rights, students'
Supreme Court of the United States, rulings of, in cases involving children's rights, 26—29, 33—44. *See also under specific case names*

Teleological arguments for denying or granting legal rights. *See* Beneficence, argument from; Utility, argument from
Teleological principles. *See* Normative principles, teleological
Terman, L. M., 70n
Tinker v. *Des Moines Independent Community School District,* 34—37
Torts, liability of child to his own, 29

Utilitarian considerations: in arguments for laws creating status offenses, 123; in arguments for neglect statutes, 134; in arguments for rehabilitating juvenile delinquents, 140–41
Utility: argument from, 76, 95; central problem encountered by argument from, 96; hedonist version of principle of, 81–82, 104—8; moral objection to use of principle of, 80; principle of, 84; principle of, distinguished from principle of beneficence, 65; principle of, distinguished from principle of justice, 96

Value: extrinsic, 105—6; hedonist theory of, 105; intrinsic, 104—5
Van Stolk, Mary, 23n, 25n

Wald, Michael, 136
White, Justice, 38, 39
Worsfold, Victor L., 88

THE JOHNS HOPKINS UNIVERSITY PRESS

This book was composed in Times Roman Quadritek text and display type by Brushwood Graphics from a design by Alan Carter. It was printed on 50-lb. Publishers Eggshell Wove by Publication Press Sales, Inc.

Library of Congress Cataloging in Publication Data

Houlgate, Laurence D
The child and the state.

Bibliography: p.
Includes index.
1. Children—Legal status, laws, etc.—
United States. 2. Parent and child (Law)—United
States. 3. Sociological jurisprudence.
4. Children—Legal status, laws, etc. I. Title.
KF479.H68 346'.73'013 79-15393
ISBN 0-8018-2288-2